WOMEN AND THE LAKES II

MORE UNTOLD GREAT LAKES MARITIME TALES

FREDERICK STONEHOUSE

AVERY COLOR STUDIOS, INC.
GWINN, MICHIGAN

©2005 Avery Color Studios, Inc.

ISBN 1-892384-30-2

Library of Congress Control Number: 2004115511

First Edition 2005

Published by
Avery Color Studios, Inc.
Gwinn, Michigan 49841

TABLE OF CONTENTS

INTRODUCTION

Like the original *Women and the Lakes, Women and the Lakes, II* is anecdotal history. It looks at events very broadly without any effort to evaluate them against measurable criteria. It does not look at trends or draw conclusions. As in *Women and the Lakes*, the book celebrates the triumph and tragedy of the individual rather than of the faceless masses.

As in *Women and the Lakes*, the stories are endless. The books only begin to scratch the surface, however, each does help to bring the experience of Great Lakes women into the light of day and better illustrate their important role in the history of the Inland Seas.

There are many untouched contemporary areas. For example, women are increasingly part of today's Coast Guard and commercial fleets. While their numbers are less than the men, they certainly are only the crest of the coming wave!

It is believed some women went "to sea" out of a sense of adventure. Others needed the money. Stonehouse Collection

1

Sometimes life on the lakes was a bit "rough and tumble." Stonehouse Collection

Historically there are several specific areas that deserve closer examination. For example, it would be valuable to learn more about the role women played in commercial fishing. Was it the same on all the Great Lakes? How did it evolve with changes in technology? Did they do every job or just specific ones? We know women were employed as "ladies maids" on some passenger steamers. How many vessels and what were their duties? A cursory examination of the material indicates in some instances a single maid was expected to take care of perhaps a hundred female passengers. As this is clearly beyond the ability of a single person, how did she make it work? What did they do in the off-season?

Certainly more work should be focused on researching the story of "Rosie the Riveter" on the Great Lakes. Like their saltwater sisters, during World War II women provided critical augmentation to the shipyards across the Great Lakes. Yards at Duluth, Superior, Manitowoc, Toledo, Sturgeon Bay and elsewhere built hundreds of vessels for the war effort. Women certainly did their share, but it is still a largely untold story.

The topic needing the least work is female lightkeepers. Their lives and times have clearly been "documented to death!" That said, I did include a lightkeeping chapter because the subject is so popular.

History is inclusive, counting the activities of all the people, their accomplishments and failures. We need to continue to explore the dark attics or musty basements of the Great Lakes story to discover the *complete* history of our Inland Seas.

CHAPTER ONE

ADVENTURES AFLOAT

Birth

It wasn't always death and shipwreck. Sometimes it was life as illustrated in this April 21, 1874 *Detroit Free Press* item.

"A BIRTH ON THE MARINE CITY–McKINLOCH'S COURTESY - Sunday evening, while the steamer *Marine City* was crossing Saginaw Bay on her trip down from Alpena, Mrs. Dust, a passenger on the boat from Alpena, gave birth to a male child. The wind was blowing fresh and a heavy sea running. Most of the ladies on the boat were sick. Mr. John McKinloch, the steward, is entitled to and received much credit for his assiduous care and attention, earning the lasting gratitude of the passengers. Both mother and child are doing well.[i]"

On August 30, 1880, the *Marine City* burned and sank a few miles north of Harrisburg, Michigan on Lake Huron. Two nearby tugs saw her distress and were able to rescue many of those aboard but still 10-20 people were killed.[ii]

Cook'n and Sail'n

Working as a cook on a Great Lakes sailing vessel was a very traditional role for women. In the 1880s it was estimated nearly a quarter of all cooks were female. In many instances they were related to the captain or mate. The early schooners were often family affairs and women took their rightful place in the enterprise. In other instances they were employees like any other member of the crew.

In some instances the woman sailed as cook to be with her husband. There were also cases where the children came along too! The captain wanted his family with him and it worked out for the best.[iii]

In the 1870s the *Chicago Inter-Ocean*, a newspaper engaged in a vigorous effort to build circulation with "sensational" reporting, started a mini-journalistic war by claiming the female cooks were nothing but water borne harlots. The paper eagerly printed stories about cooks running away with captains and mates, "stealing" the men from their loyal wives ashore. Letters to the editor flooded the paper taking both sides of the "issue." Some were purportedly written by ship owners, captains, mates, wives and cooks. I suspect many were "ghosted" by *Chicago Inter-Ocean* writers.

In truth the great majority of the cooks were hard working women struggling to make a living, not any different than a male crewman. However there often was a pay differential with the female coming out the worse. Although the evidence is somewhat spotty, captains and owners did try to pay the women less than a man doing the same job. In 1873 captains and owners resolved to pay male cooks $30 a month and females $20. By contrast ten years later in Chicago female cooks were getting a bounty over the men, the captains wanting only females! While we can conclude women cooks usually received less than the men, it was not always so.[iv]

Cooking on a Great Lakes sailing vessel was hard work under difficult conditions. It wasn't the place for a purring sex kitten looking for love on the high seas.

The cook was up by dawn and soon had a fire going in the galley wood stove. Heavy pots and pans were heating on the burners and breakfast for the crew was well under way. All the time the galley was moving as the ship danced and jumped with the movement of the waves. More than one cook suffered severe burns as a pot of boiling something spilled onto her. There was no "pre prepared" food. Everything was made from scratch and the crew expected fresh biscuits in the morning and warm bread for dinner. Dishes, silverware, pots and pans had to be cleaned too. Cook'n and sail'n was a tough job.

Although trying to characterize the female cook is virtually impossible, it can be suggested that she was likely a country girl used to doing everything that needed doing without complaint. She was most likely stoutly built which was important to be able to handle the heavy work and her hands were large and red from the character of the work and harsh cleaners. Her personality had to be "strong" to be able to handle the mix and tumble of shipboard life.

At least some of the cooks were known to chew tobacco, smoke cigars, spit, drink and swear as well as any of the sailors. It was a tough life and needed tough women.

There certainly were cases where crew (including the captain) tried to force themselves on a cook. How common this was is unknown. The evidence is mostly anecdotal. In 1880, several crewmen raped the cook on a schooner in Portsmouth, near Kingston on Lake Ontario.[v] In 1882 the "soused up" master of the schooner *Midland Rover* fired his handgun at the female cook.[vi] Perhaps the eggs were too "runny!"

During the great age of passenger vessels on the lakes, women were frequently employed in traditional roles of maids and stewardesses. Stonehouse Collection

7

Cook or Crew

Not all women on a sailing vessel wanted to cook. As this item from the April 15, 1872 *Oswego Palladium* indicates.

"About half past one this afternoon, foot passengers on the lower bridge, were attracted by the cries of murder, which emanated from the cabin of the schooner *Cape Horn* lying outside of Doolittle's pier. Hundreds flocked to the scene, but before reaching it they saw the Captain, Ben Oyster, and the cook, Mrs. Jones, a lady (!) from Kingston, emerge from the companionway, and engage in fierce combat on the deck, abaft the cabin.

"Mrs. Jones had decidedly the best of the fight, armed as she was with the first class fit out of a "galley," which she was hurling at the captain's head with such perfect abandon, as shows her to be adept in the art of serving, if not cooking with a large iron kettle, she felled the captain to the deck, and was only prevented from bashing his brains out, by the interference of outsiders.

"Both were looking very badly, with their torn and disordered garments and blood streaming from their heads. The captain's cuts are quite severe, and called for dressing by a surgeon. Officer Hogan was promptly on hand and arrested both parties.

"We learn that the cause of the difficulty was, that the woman did not want to cook, but rather to sail the vessel, and to this the captain objected. This noon Mrs. Jones went ashore, and the captain put her trunk, band-box, jockey hat and feather on the dock. This was too much to see that darling hat exposed to vulgar view and on the dock, at that she went for the captain. The Recorder will quell the mutiny. The matter was settled at the Police Court by the Captain paying Mrs. Jones $14."[vii]

Trapped

Being involved in shipwreck is certainly a terrifying event. But being trapped inside of a capsized vessel is beyond description. Women were involved in at least two such incidents.

In September 1855 the small schooner *Experiment* was on Lake Michigan bound from Chicago to St. Joseph, Michigan. The 65-foot long schooner was built in St. Joseph the pervious year and was considered a fine vessel.

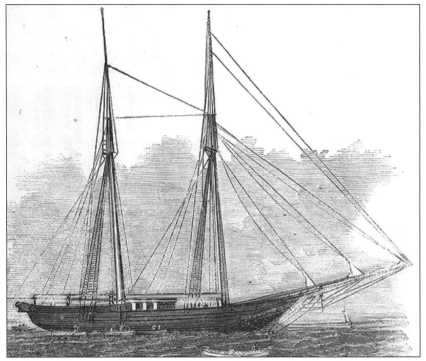

The schooner S.J. Waring *was very similar to the* Experiment.
Stonehouse Collection

Other than Captain Jennings and his four-man crew, the schooner carried Mrs. Henrietta Napier and her two children, 15-year-old Edward and 10 month-old Hardin. As the schooner approached St. Joseph, a sudden gale capsized her, trapping Henrietta and her children as well as a sailor, in the cabin. Captain Jennings and his men above decks were swept away. Luckily for those in the cabin, an air pocket formed when she rolled, allowing them to breath, otherwise death would have been quick. But the situation was horrible. They were trapped in a very small cabin with everything turned upside down. It was utterly black, without any illumination at all. Water sloshed around their chests and they knew at anytime the schooner could plunge to the bottom of the lake, dragging all to their death. In the struggle to stay above water in the cabin, the baby slipped from Henrietta's arms and disappeared forever into the cold black water.

After what must have seemed like an eternity, the *Experiment* drifted onto a sandbar near the St. Joseph harbor entrance. Intrigued by the wreck, several local residents started to explore her. Hearing voices and the sound of people climbing on the hull, Henrietta and her companions yelled and pounded on the ship in a desperate effort to attract attention. It worked. Soon a hole was chopped through the hull and the victims released. It was said the terrible ordeal, especially the loss of her infant, tormented Henrietta for the rest of her life.

The schooner was repaired and returned to service, eventually wrecking at the entrance to St. Joseph harbor on September 12, 1902. Ironically the loss occurred in nearly the same location the hull drifted on to the bar so many years before. She was inbound to St. Joseph in a southwest gale when she swerved to avoid an obstruction and went out of control. The local life-saving crew removed her crew of six but the old schooner was a total loss. [viii]

A very similar disaster happened in 1859 on Lake Erie. The big 160-foot bark *Sunshine* departed Buffalo for Saginaw, Michigan on Lake Huron on June 30. Captain Cornelius McNeil commanded the bark and had a crew of 11 plus his wife Persilla and their three children. The *Sunshine* was still on Lake Erie on July 2 when Persilla became seasick and stayed in her cabin. Without warning a "white squall" or sudden gale blasted into the bark and in spite of the crew's attempts to strike sail, the *Sunshine* capsized. Because Lake Erie is so shallow, averaging only 60-odd feet deep, when she rolled, the masts hit bottom, knocking them away. Freed of her top hamper, the bark slowly came back up to her beam-ends and wallowed in the rolling seas. Several men were lost when she first went over. Others when the seas inundated the wreck. Six of the crew led by the second mate, survived by hanging on to what solid pieces of the ship they could find. Initially they thought Persilla and her children were lost in the roll over but this wasn't true.

When the bark capsized, she and the children were trapped in the cabin as in the *Experiment* disaster. The cabin was utterly black. Imagine the terrible situation. One second all is normal and the next second everything is upside down and water is sweeping into the cabin from everywhere! Fortunately the cabin table was bolted to the floor, which was now the roof and allowed the table to be used as an ad hoc shelf for the trapped family to hold on to. When the bark rolled up to a beam ends position, they all were dumped back into the water.

Once things settled down a bit, the men topside heard banging from the cabin and realizing what had likely happened, frantically tore away the bulkhead allowing them to escape. However Persilla was the only survivor. When the vessel rolled back up, throwing everyone in the cabin into the water again, the three children drowned! The distraught mother was dressed only in her sleeping gown and each man provided her with an item of clothing to help her survive the cold. The schooner *Nebraska* sighted the wreck the next morning and the half dead survivors were rescued.

Eventually the tug *Relief* brought her into port where she was salvaged and rebuilt. The *Sunshine* capsized again in 1871 killing most of her crew. Salvaged, she sailed until November 1906 when she was lost in a fire in Detroit.[ix]

West Side

Another shipwreck tale involved the small schooner *West Side*. As you read this short item from the October 30, 1906 *Detroit Free Press*, consider the thoughts the mother must have had, battling the storm with her entire family around her! Also consider that another woman owned the schooner.

SCHR. *WEST SIDE* IS LOST

———

Capt. Youngs, Wife and Three Sons Battle in Small Boat Many Hours

———

PORT HURON FAMILY MADE UP THE CREW

———

Little Schooner, Bound for Delray with Pulpwood, Caught in Lake Huron

———

After being buffeted about by the heavy seas of Lake Huron from Saturday night until Monday morning, Capt. Youngs, his wife and three sons, of Port Huron, composing the crew of the little schooner *West Side*, were rescued from a small boat by the big steel steamer *Frank Peavey* and landed at Port Huron last night.

Bound from Tobermoray (sic), Georgian Bay, to Delray* with pulpwood, the small schooner was caught in the severe gale of Saturday, and is believed by the captain and his family to have been lost about twenty-five miles off Thunder Bay Island, Lake Huron.

There was no opportunity for the schooner to find shelter, as it was on the wrong side of the lake, when considered with reference to the direction the gale was blowing.

The father and master of the boat, with his three sons, made heroic efforts to bring the schooner through the storm, but were finally defeated by the gale, and compelled to launch the yawl boat. This was a perilous undertaking in the seas, which were running, but it was successfully accomplished. Then the struggle to keep afloat was renewed.

All suffered greatly from exposure, but after several hours on the *Peavey*, were brought around again. The quintet of mariners landed in a small boat of the Lynn reporting agency, late last night. It is stated that the ages of the sons ranged from about ten years to eighteen years.

According to the marine directories the schooner *West Side* is owned by Bertha Dahlke, of Cleveland, and was built in 1870. It measures 138 feet long and 26 feet beam.

So far as known, no loss of life has resulted from the gale. The loss of the schooner *Vienna*, and other storm news, will be found in the marine columns.[x]

*Now part of Detroit.

Argo

While many women were lost by shipwreck, others survived by remarkable rescue. Early on the morning of November 24, 1905 the passenger steamer *Argo* was approaching Holland Harbor bound from Chicago. A 50 mile per hour north gale had whipped Lake Michigan into a frenzy and rather than try to make the harbor entrance under such terrible condition, her captain decided to lay

The crew of the Holland, Michigan, Life-Saving Station standing by their lifeboat. Stonehouse Collection

off for a bit to see if the wind dropped. At 5:30 a.m. it seemed the gale decreased a little and conscious of his schedule, he headed into Holland. The gap through the north and south breakwater piers was narrow but he had run it safely many times before under equally difficult conditions. Not this time! As he drew up to the gap a wave pushed the stern to port and the *Argo* smashed hard into the north pier. Quickly another wave drove her off the rocks and on to a sand bar 500 feet off shore. Although she was a well-built steel vessel, the powerful waves soon started to break her.

The U.S. Life-Saving Station crew at Holland reacted quickly and attempted to reach the wreck in their surfboat but the breaking waves were too strong. It was also impossible for the *Argo* to use any of her lifeboats because of the terrible storm conditions. Aboard the steamer were 19 passengers and a crew of 22. Without rescue they were lost!

The U.S. Life-Saving station at Holland performed in many rescues.
Stonehouse Collection

Incapable of quitting, by temperament and regulation, the Life-Saving crew used their Lyle gun to fire a light shot line to the *Argo.* Considering the distance off shore the wreck was and the need to place the gun out of the reach of the waves, it was a very long shot. Under normal conditions the maximum range of the gun was 400 yards. Keeper Chauncey D. Pool carefully aimed his gun, gauged the wind, and pulled the firing lanyard. With a sharp crack the 19-pound projectile trailing its light shot line flew towards the *Argo* and landed just past her, dropping the line neatly across the deck. Quickly the steamer's sailors used the light line to haul a one-inch whip line out with its block, lashing the pulley to the mast. Ashore the life-savers used the whip to haul out the heavy two-inch hawser and breeches buoy. The last item was nothing more than a round life ring with a set of heavy canvas trousers sewn onto it. Suspended by a block and rope harness arrangement from the big hawser and made fast to the whip line, it enabled those aboard the ship to be pulled to shore one at a time. It was a critical piece of life-saving equipment.

Once the beach apparatus was rigged and ready to go, it was just a case of waiting for someone to get in it. Doubtless the people on

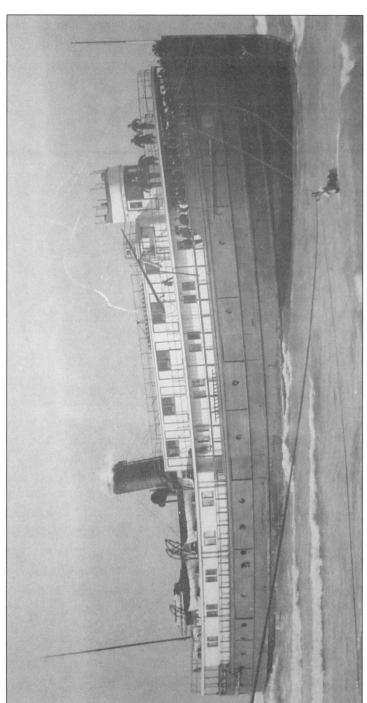

The lifeline dips into Lake Michigan while a victim is hauled ashore. Stonehouse Collection

the wreck looked at crashing waves and very narrow rope running from ship to shore as well as the strange breeches buoy and considered whether it was better to stay with the ship than risk their lives to such a flimsy looking contraption!

Eventually one of the women, Mrs. C.E. Johnson of Big Rapids, Michigan gathered up her courage and climbed in. On signal the Life-Savers ashore hauled away and she went bouncing off, swaying wildly above the surging waves until the breeches buoy reached the beach. Taking the ride next was Mrs. W. P. Canaan of Grand Rapids. She must have been more "substantial" than Mrs. Johnson since midway across the hawser bellied low into the surf, giving her a good dousing. One observer claimed she was more under water than above it. But above all, she was safe ashore. Her ten-year-old daughter was next and she certainly had the ride of her life, laughing all the way! Her husband had the most trouble of all. Halfway ashore the rope broke at the mast, sending him crashing into the water. Quickly the Life-Savers managed to pull him to safety like fish on a line. After a new rope was rigged the remainder of the crew and passengers safely came ashore. The Life-Savers even managed to bring a large gray horse belonging to the Grand Rapids Fire Department to shore. They fastened ropes to his harness, pushed him into the water, and hauled him to the beach without injury.[xi]

Bruno and *Louisa*

The experience of the female cook on the steamer *Bruno* was more harrowing than that of her *Argo* sisters. The 136-foot wooden steamer *Bruno* and her consort, the old schooner *Louisa*, left Cleveland on November 1, 1890 upbound with coal. Having a steamer tow a schooner was a good way to increase the efficiency of both vessels. When they were off Thunder Bay Island they were overtaken by a strong southeast gale and building sea. The two vessels fought their way along for a full day until they both hit infamous Magnetic Reef on Georgian Bay. Now things rapidly went from bad to worse with waves sweeping over both decks. The *Louisa* lost both hatch covers to the powerful seas and finally a monster wave washed her entire deck cabin away! Another wave took her lifeboat off into the black night. The crew of five men and a female cook climbed into the rigging, lashed themselves tight and hung on for their lives as the angry waves surged mere feet below them. Things were a little better on the steamer. Only part of her cabin was lost and the 11-man crew huddled in what little structure remained. For thirty hours both crews fought for their lives. Finally the gale calmed and the *Bruno's* lifeboat was launched, carrying everyone to safety at Cockburn Island, five long miles distant. Eventually a tug was secured and all survivors delivered to Toronto, but it had been a very near thing.[xii]

Onoko

Sometimes escape was more matter of a normal activity than especially dangerous but certainly leaving any sinking ship is an adventure.

When Cleveland's Globe Shipbuilding Works launched *Onoko* in 1882 she was both the first iron freighter built on the Great Lakes and the largest vessel of any kind on the Inland Seas. With an overall length of 302 feet and beam of 39 feet she could carry 110, 000 bushels of wheat or 3,000 tons of iron ore, massive loads for the time. By contrast a modern 1,000-foot Great Lakes freighter today can haul more than 60,000 tons depending on channel depth. The *Onoko* is important because she is the historic prototype for the fleets of bulk freighters that would soon follow. These distinctive vessels were critical for the cheap transportation of bulk cargo, including iron ore, grain, coal and stone.

She had a relatively uneventful career until September 15, 1915. She had just loaded a full cargo of corn in Duluth and was downbound about 25 miles out when the engineer saw a deluge of water flooding into the engine room from somewhere beneath the machinery. Since the pumps couldn't keep up with the flow, all Captain W.R. Dunn could do was order abandon ship. The *Onoko* was heading for the bottom and there wasn't anything any of the crew could do about it.

The crew of 16 and one passenger left her in the lifeboat and within minutes the old freighter disappeared beneath the waves.

The Onoko *was the first iron freighter built on the Great Lakes.*
Stonehouse Collection

The lone woman aboard was Mrs. C.R. Cranbee, the wife of the steward. She was just cleaning up from lunch when the frantic call was made to head for the lifeboat. Had she waited just a few more minutes she could have left the dirty dishes! The water was calm and soon they were picked up by the Standard Oil steamer *Renown* and returned to Duluth.

The cause of the sinking was believed to be a "dropped" hull plate. The *Onoko* had grounded briefly when leaving the grain elevator after loading and it is surmised she damaged the hull at that time.[xiii]

This remarkable series of photos shows the Onoko *on the way down.*
Stonehouse Collection

Whip

In contrast to Lydia Dale and the heartless crew of the *Hartzell*, the captain of the schooner *Whip* made an extraordinary and courageous effort to save his cook to the point of losing his own life.

On March 21, 1865, the schooner departed St. Joseph bound for Chicago with a cargo of lumber. Soon after reaching the open lake she was hammered by a west gale. Seeing no reason in trying to battle his way through the storm, captain Nelson H. Blend came about and headed back to St. Joseph. When the storm increased in violence the crew lashed themselves to the rigging to prevent being washed away by waves sweeping over her deck. The female cook was sent below for her safety.

Getting back to the harbor was not an easy maneuver. The wind and waves drove the schooner too far to the north and she went aground about a quarter mile north of the harbor entrance. Water began to flood into the hold and realizing his cook could drown in the deluge, Captain Blend untied himself and headed across the open deck to the companionway. Halfway to his goal he was swept overboard and into the boiling lake to his death.

After watching the disaster from shore, some sailors used a yawl to go out to the wreck and rescue the remaining men. They discovered the cook still in her cabin below decks and in water up to her chin. They hauled her up to the deck and to eventual safety ashore.

The captain's death was a terrible loss not only for the friends of this noble man, but also for his wife and six small children.[xiv]

Hattie Wells

All women afloat were not victims of shipwreck. Sometimes they were considered heroes. A case in point is the *Hattie Wells*.

The *Wells* was originally built as a schooner in 1867. During her life she suffered her share of scrapes and bumps with an occasional shipwreck thrown in for good measure. By 1912 she was reduced to a simple barge.

In early November of that year she was under tow of the tug *James H. Martin* bound from Waukegan, Illinois for Muskegon with a cargo of lumber. Midway across the lake a gale blew up strong enough to send waves sweeping across the old vessels deck. When the donkey engine used to power her pumps failed, the *Wells* was in deep trouble. No longer could she pump the water out of her flooding cargo holds.

In an effort to save his charge, the tug captain decided to run for South Haven but the gale was too strong and halfway between there and St. Joseph the old *Wells* was getting ready to take the final plunge. The *Martin* dropped the hawser to the *Wells* and attempted to lay alongside to allow the five-man crew to jump to safety. The heaving seas, with one vessel plunging into the trough while the other soared to heavens made the difficult operation impossible. If the captain of the tug misjudged the maneuver in the slightest, his ship would be smashed to kindling and all persons would be lost.

Instead he ran as close to the sinking *Wells* as he dared and a sailor heaved a rope to the barge. One by one the *Wells* sailors tied off to the rope and were hauled to the tug like fish. All were saved.

What isn't often mentioned in this shipwreck tale is the role played by the two teenaged stewardesses aboard the tug. Margaret LaJoyce and Elizabeth DeBeck were continuously on deck throughout the rescue, urging the tug men to make every effort to save the *Wells* men. They knew the danger but also knew no fear. The tug crew couldn't do anything but their best with such cheerleaders.[xv]

CHAPTER TWO

DEATH ON THE LAKE

Hurricane Disaster

Sailor's wives always had the melancholy duty of handling the problems shipwreck death left behind. Perhaps the family had enough money saved to survive or relations that could provide shelter until she was able to get set up on her own. Likely the worst duty of all was to recover the body and bring it home for burial.

During a screaming west gale on November 24, 1860 a large black schooner was driven ashore about eight miles north of St. Joseph, Michigan on Lake Michigan. The schooner didn't last long. By the following day the pounding waves smashed her to pieces. Only the wheat cast on the sand gave mute testimony to her cargo. The lifeless body of a crewman washing to and fro in the heaving surf gave silent evidence the crew was gone too.

Eventually it was discovered she was the *Hurricane* bound from Chicago to Buffalo, with 14,000 bushels of wheat. Her captain was young William Walch and he sailed with a crew of nine. Eventually the victims came silently ashore, borne by the same waves they planned would carry them home to Buffalo.

About a week after the wreck was identified, a sad young woman arrived in St. Joseph. She was the widow of the *Hurricane's* captain and had arrived to bring her husband home.[xvi]

Lydia Dale and the *Hartzell*

As the "weaker" gender, women were expected to be "protected" by men. In the event of shipwreck, the call was supposed to be, at least in popular literature, "women and children first." Note, women came before children! In real life, it often didn't work out that way as illustrated by the case of the schooner *J.H. Hartzell* on October 16, 1880.

The schooner was bound down from Lake Superior with a cargo of iron ore for the Frankfort Furnace Company, in Frankfort, Michigan on the west shore of Lake Michigan. Aboard were six men and the female cook, Lydia Dale. The cook joined the schooner in Buffalo but was said to hail from Toledo. By all accounts, Lydia was a good cook and well thought of by everyone. The trip was uneventful and the *Hartzell* arrived off Frankfort about 3: 00 a.m. on Saturday the 16th. The captain decided rather than run directly into a port he was not very well familiar with in the dark, he would lay off until daylight. It was a fateful decision.

Around 6:00 a.m. the wind veered southwest from southeast and began to blow a hard gale. Squalls of hail, snow and rain lashed the schooner. She was two miles or so south of the channel piers when the shift happened and although the captain tried to work further off shore, the wind drove him landward. When it became plain he could make no progress, the captain dropped both anchors and sig-naled distress. The anchors failed to hold and the schooner drifted in toward shore until going hard up on the middle bar about three hundred yards from the beach. The shore opposite was very difficult, with sand bluffs several hundred feet high running nearly to the water's edge. It was a terrible place for a shipwreck!

The building seas worked the schooner over. The yawl was soon carried away and the waves washed regularly over her wooden decks battering her cabins. All the crew could do was climb the rigging and lash themselves in. This was easy enough for healthy men to do, but Lydia had been seriously ill with a high fever for several days and very weak. It took the full efforts of four sailors to hoist her prostrate form to safety on the cross trees of the foremast across which planks were nailed as a platform for her. Bundled tightly in several blankets with sailcloth as an outside weather shield, she waited for rescue with the men. Her head rested on a sailor's knee.

Soon after the crew fled aloft the over stressed mainmast toppled into the lake leaving the foremast to sway ominously in the screaming wind. It seemed it would soon go over too.

Help however was on the way. A sharp-eyed fisherman's son spotted the schooner shortly after she went up on the bar and alerted the towns people of the wreck. One group of citizens went to the beach opposite the wreck and built a roaring bonfire and laid driftwood on the base of the bluff to spell, "life-boat coming" as signals to the crew to take heart, help was on the way.

Another man galloped on horseback to the nearest Life-Saving Service station, 10 miles distant at Point au Bec Scies. While ten miles may not seem very far, under the circumstances it was distant indeed. No roads connected the station with Frankfort. The crew would have to bring their equipment through the wilderness.

Station keeper Thomas E. Matthews immediately ordered out his beach apparatus complete with Lyle gun, breeches buoy, hawser and hauling lines and other equipment. Using the horse from Frankfort to pull the cart, Matthews and his crew set out with all speed.

At times the terrain was so difficult both horse and men could barely pull the cart 10 or 15 yards without stopping and resting. The cart with all of its gear weighed more than a thousand pounds. The gear was critically important if the crew of the schooner was to be saved. All the while the life-savers were working their way to the wreck; they were constantly assaulted by the storm. The icy wind tore through the trees and rain and hail alternately lashed them. The men were wet and half-frozen but there was a job to do. When the horse went lame, the crew dragged the cart themselves.

Sometimes they had to stop to clear the way of brush and fallen trees. Eventually a team of horses from Frankfort met them and took over the greater pulling burden while a group of citizens armed with saws and axes worked to clear a rough trail. It was still murderous going. Eventually they reached the bluff high above the wreck and looked down on the terrible tempest in full fury. Keeper Matthews had his men use the one-inch whip-line to lower the cart down the bluff to a narrow precipice 10 or 12 feet wide and a couple of hundred feet below the ridge. When the line ran out, the crew and accompanying citizens cast it loose from the belaying tree at the top of the bluff and just grabbed on to it. Digging their heels into the soft sand, they slowed the descent of the cart with their own weight, frequently being dragged along behind. Eventually they reached the small plateau.

Acting from years of training, the life-savers were soon ready to shoot. The first shot was perfect, dropping the line across the *Hartzell*. Although the captain quickly grabbed it, the powerful waves swept it under the wreck where it fouled. The life-savers hauled it back ashore, flaked it in the prescribed method on the ground so it would not foul when shot, and carefully aimed the Lyle gun again, increasing the power charge to compensate for the heavier, wet and sand filled shotline. Again the little gun fired, again dropping the shotline over the crosstrees where the sailors grabbed it. Hand over hand the men pulled the light line until finally the bight of the whip-line and tail block appeared and was made fast to the mast. Using the whip line, the crew ashore hauled the heavy two-inch hawser out and the sailors made it fast to the mast. The breeches buoy was quickly rigged on the rope ashore and run out to the wreck.

Carefully one of the sailors lowered himself into the breeches buoy and signaled he was ready. Working under the keeper's direction, the local townspeople, estimated at 50-60, hauled on the whip line and brought him ashore. The sailor turned out to be the mate, John Cassidy. Asked why the woman didn't come ashore first as expected, he explained she was afraid to get in the breeches buoy. This revelation and the determination that the weakened mast could be pulled over by the stress of the tight breeches buoy rope, caused the keeper to change to the lifecar. This device looked like a small covered metal boat perhaps seven feet long. Attached to the hawser in the same manner as the breeches buoy, it was pulled out to the wreck through the waves and then tight to the bitter end of the rope. Up to four victims could climb inside and after securing a small metal hatch behind them, were pulled to safety ashore. Although more cumbersome than a breeches buoy, it was faster and

It was a lifecar like this one that brought the survivors, except Lydia Dale, safely ashore. Stonehouse Collection

in a situation as faced by the life-savers, a perfect tool to bring the *Hartzell* victims to the beach.

The life-savers immediately switched the buoy for the lifecar and hauled it out to the wreck where it hung vertically from the crosstrees. Two men were seen to cautiously climb down from their perch in the rigging and enter the car. A third man secured the door and the lifecar was hauled to the beach. After reaching shore the men were questioned about why the cook didn't come but gave evasive answers. All the life-savers could do was send the lifecar out again.

The life-savers watched eagerly as the lifecar reached the wreck and was slowly pulled up to the crosstrees. In the official report the Life-Saving Service noted, "The captain of the sunken vessel meanwhile crept up from his place in the lower rigging toward the men above. He was so exhausted by long standing and exposure that he was unable to climb over the futtock-shrouds on the crosstrees and was prevented from ascending through the orifice which had been left in the platform, as the lower limbs of the woman, swathed in the wrappings of the canvas, hung through the opening. By the efforts of the sailors, aided by his own, the inert body was drawn away and lashed by the bent knees to the Jacob's ladder. He then mounted through the opening and endeavored, as he testifies, to rouse the woman into some signs of life. The life-car soon hung again in mid-air below them, and the second mate and captain clambered slowly down and got in. In the beginning of the creeping darkness the car arrived from the sea and was torn open by a dozen eager hands. The crowd was confident that the woman would be brought this time and were stupefied when only the two men appeared. There was an instant burst of fierce interrogations, to which the captain and mate appear, like their predecessors, to have rendered equivocal answers. The effect of their replies was that the woman was the same as dead and that she would be or might be, brought ashore at the next trip. These rejoinders were received with sullen looks and angry murmurs from the crowd. There was no time however, for parley, as approaching night was fast darkening the storm and the two men were lead to a team nearby which drove away with them, while the life-car was hastily repaired and once more hauled upon its way."[xvii]

Keeper Matthews had the car hauled out again to the wreck. He watched carefully in the gathering night as it was brought up to the crosstrees. His glasses showed shadowy figures moving around the car, but not what they were doing or who they were. Unable to see what was happening he left the car a very long time at the wreck to provide the greatest opportunity for the men to manhandle the unconscious woman into it. It took the keeper's full powers of command to keep the crowd from pulling the life car to shore too quickly. Finally he judged he could wait no longer since the mast could fall at any time. He ordered the men to haul the lifecar to shore.

Within minutes the lifecar reached the shore. The crowd rushed forward waist deep in the waves and manhandled it to the beach. Instantly the hatch was flung open and two men climbed out, a sailor and the captain (of the schooner). There was no one else. Immediately the cry arose.

"Where's the woman?" Quickly the crowd answered itself with the angry response, "They haven't brought the woman!" The *Annual Report* picked up the situation. "The announcement was received with a savage burst of imprecations.[xviii] The dark air responded with a roar of curses and amidst the clamor men were heard yelling that they never would have laid a hand on the hauling lines if they had known that the woman was to be left on the wreck to perish. Amidst the turmoil the keeper took aside the sailor, George Hyde and asked him right in the eyes, "Why didn't you bring that woman?" Hyde faced him and replied, "The woman is dead." "Be careful now," retorted the keeper. If you don't know for certain that she's dead, say so; and if you do know, say so." "The woman is dead and stiff as a board," returned the sailor, adding, "She's been dead for sometime." The keeper then wheeled about to the sailor Coursie and sternly demanded, "Is that woman dead?" Coursie replied, "Oh yes; she's been dead for quite a while."

Keeper Matthews considered sending out the lifecar with two of his men in it to bring Lydia ashore. However in the darkness it would be impossible to tell when car reached the wreck. More important perhaps, the mast could fall at any moment. What was the value in risking the lives of two of his men to recover the body of a woman the sailors claimed was dead? Reluctantly he dismissed his men until morning. At first light he would reassess the situation. At dawn the schooner had broken up and nothing was left of her. She was all gone.

What really happened to Lydia is unknown, but her desertion evoked strong feelings in Frankfort. The townspeople believed there was no doubt the sailors left her alive on the crosstrees to more easily save their own skins. They abandoned a shipmate to a cold and lonely death. Seventeen days later Lydia's body washed ashore. A coroner's jury determined she died by drowning. Clearly the inference was she was left alive on the mast and drowned when it fell into the lake.

In defense of the sailors however, if Lydia was unconscious in the crosstrees, 60-feet above the deck, manhandling her into a lifecar would have been extremely difficult. She was a "heavy" woman, the sailors stiff, half frozen and dead tired. For them to get such a difficult burden down from the trees and through a small hatch may have been beyond their diminished capability. Saying she was already dead was just an admission of the obvious future if not present.

Regardless of facts or rationalizations, to the good folk of Frankfort, Lydia Dale was left to die high in the crosstrees of the schooner *J. H. Hartzell* by her heartless shipmates.[xix]

The storm that sunk the *Hartzell* was a devastating one. On Lake Michigan alone 94 vessels were sunk or damaged and an estimated 118 people lost their lives. 60-100 alone went down when the big side-wheeler *Alpena* "went missing."[xx]

Arcadia

The loss of the 191-foot wooden steamer *Arcadia* is still unexplained. She departed from Manistee, Michigan on April 13, 1907 bound for Two Rivers, Wisconsin with a load of hardwood.[xxi] Also aboard were 14 passengers and crew. A storm blew up and she never made safe harbor at Two Rivers, or anywhere else.

About a week later the body of her young cook, identity unknown, washed ashore at Big Sable Point, just to the south of Manistee. Whatever happened, happened soon after her departure. Other wreckage drifted on to the beach too. But none shed a clue towards why the *Arcadia* was lost.

In mid-July the body of Mrs. Harry May, the captain's wife, came ashore six miles north from the Grand Pointe Au Sable Life-Saving Station. Positive identification was only made from her clothing. This was only 13 miles north of where the cook came ashore reinforcing the theory of the loss of the vessel nearby. No other bodies were ever recovered.

The lonely life-saving service beach patrol found many shipwreck victims.
Stonehouse Collection

The mystery of the small steamer remained until the Armistice Day Storm of 1940. Following the storm, the remains of a wooden steamer were located on a sandbar off Big Point Sable. Marine men claimed the measurements matched those of the *Arcadia*. So was the mystery solved or is it just a tantalizing false lead?[xxii]

Dean Richmond

For many years one of the great "went missing" tales of Lake Erie was the propeller *Dean Richmond*. The 238-foot wooden vessel departed Toledo bound for Buffalo with a cargo of lead, zinc, copper sheets, flour and agricultural tools on October 13, 1893. Some sources even claim she carried boxes of gold coins as part of a bank transfer. Also aboard were between 16-18 people. The records are contradictory as to the correct number. Among them was Mrs. Rita Ellsworth of Alymer, Ontario. She was the stewardess and responsible for feeding the men.

After Toledo, Captain Stoddard swung the *Dean Richmond* eastward and through the always treacherous Pelee Passage and into open Lake Erie. The storm winds were blowing hard and rapidly building into what some considered the worst weather to hit the lake in a long time. Soon winds in excess of 70 miles per hour accompanied by sheets of rain were tearing at the vessel. Tossed to and fro, she continued to battle the gale. On the morning of October 14 the captain of the steamer *Helena* sighted her off Long Point on the Canadian side of the lake. She was in obvious trouble. Around noon the captain of the steamer *Neshoto* saw her in the same area but now one of her two stacks was missing. Without the stack, boiler draft was gone and therefore one of the two engines disabled. Captain Stoddard must have turned to try to run for Dunkirk, New York since around dusk the captain of the steamer *W. H. Stevens* sighted her about four miles east of Erie. As he watched her battle the terrible storm the remaining stack fell, leaving her helpless in the tempest. Unable to render any aid in the storm, the *Stevens* left the propeller to her lonely fate.

The following morning residents in the area found their beach littered with wreckage from the steamer. Sacks and barrels of flour, cabin woodwork and related flotsam lay on the beach and washed around in the breakers. One farmer was said to have salvaged over 2,000 sacks of flour! Certainly the propeller had sunk off Dunkirk, perhaps shortly after the *Stevens* sighting. Later in the day the bodies came ashore. More came in the night too. All were wearing life jackets. The local coroner stated the victims died from exposure. None had drowned. Like so many sailors before and after, it wasn't water that killed them but the terrible cold. The captain's and mate's watches had stopped at 12:20 a.m. leading to the conclusion the ship broke up shortly before midnight, October 14. Among the bodies was the stewardess, Rita Ellsworth.

For reasons that are unclear but perhaps can be blamed on nothing more than a warped desire for attention, the morning following the wreck a man calling himself C.L. Clark was found wandering on the beach. He claimed to be a survivor of the wreck, stating that he was aboard her when she broke up and lost his

Stewardess Rita Ellsworth disappeared with the Dean Richmond. Stonehouse Collection

memory until he woke up on the beach. While he related many "facts" of the loss that seemed plausible, he claimed the captain's wife and three children were also aboard her and doubtless their presence influenced the captain's decisions. He was exposed as a hoax when the captain's wife arrived in Dunkirk to claim his body.

The storm that sank the *Dean Richmond* wasn't confined to Lake Erie. It is claimed approximately 100 Great Lakes vessels were wrecked in the storm.

The *Dean Richmond* became one of Lake Erie's "went missing" ships, vessels that sank and were never found. Many claimed they "knew" her location and several even attempted to salvage her, doubtlessly fueled by the rumors of gold. However the wreck was always a ghost, avoiding discovery. In 1982 she finally succumbed to Gary Kozak and his side scan sonar search. There was no gold, only lowly lead and zinc but another great mystery was finally solved.[xxiii]

C.O.D.

In an accident reminiscent of the terrible *Hartzell* disaster near Frankfort, Michigan on Lake Michigan another female cook met a lonely death in a schooners rigging. The schooner *C.O.D.* was bound from Port Huron on Lake Huron for Buffalo with a cargo of wheat when she was blown on to a sandbar three miles east of Port Burwell, Ontario, Lake Erie, on October 22, 1887.

When the schooner began to break up the crewmen abandoned her and were able to swim through the breakers to safety. The female cook however was unable to do this. Perhaps she was too modest, unwilling to remove her voluminous clothing and strip down or was just physically too weak to make the desperate attempt. In any case, the men left her lashed to the rigging where she died alone likely frozen to death by the frigid fall winds.[xxiv]

Capsized

A very early accident in Canadian waters claimed a woman crossing from Wolfe Island to Kingston, Ontario via a small ferry. On November 28 (or 25) the small ferry was crossing in rough seas with 11 persons aboard and a cargo of 25 bushels of wheat. When a heavy wave hit the craft the wheat shifted to one side and she went over and all aboard ended up in the water. Immediately sailors from other boats went to their aid and were able to save nine. But a Mr. Shannon and his wife were lost. It was likely a case of heavy period dress dooming the poor woman.[xxv]

Consumed by Fire

Another example of the male crew escaping but somehow leaving the female cook behind happened on the small 115-foot propeller *Sea Gull* in July 1890. The schooner was moored at Bearinger's Dock in East Tawas, Michigan, Lake Huron, when she was discovered ablaze at 1:00 a.m. Within minutes the roaring flames spread to the dock piled high with 5 million feet of pine lumber and soon it was burning too! When the *Sea Gull's* lines burned through she floated to another dock piled with 7 million feet of lumber. Soon this too was ablaze. She continued on to a third dock with 4 million feet that also caught fire. Eventually she drifted onto a lonely beach and burned to the water's edge. The actual cause of the fire is not known. It could have been galley related or even an overturned lantern.

It is interesting that the entire crew of the *Sea Gull* safely abandoned her with the first cry of fire except for the female cook. Why she was trapped aboard is unknown. Was it a case of no one bothering to wake her since her quarters were separate from the men or was she already overcome by smoke or flame? Did she delay from a false sense of modesty... perhaps, "I can't let anyone see me like this."[xxvi]

The *Eastland* Women

Many women have perished on Great Lakes shipwrecks. Certainly the loss of the steamer *Eastland* in Chicago in July 24, 1915 was the cause of the greatest female lives in a single incident. Of the 841 people reported killed, 436 were women.[xxvii]

The *Eastland* was built in Port Huron, Michigan in 1903 for the Michigan Steamship Company. The ship failed to meet her speed guarantee and had to be modified with induced draft to increase power. An air conditioning system was also added to help solve a problem with internal air circulation in her cabins. Both modifications unfortunately increased the ship's tendency to be top heavy. Reportedly several times during her career she developed unanticipated lists requiring the crew to quickly counter flood ballast tanks to right the ship. Rumors about her instability were common on the lakes.

The *Eastland* went through several owners and different ports of call and by 1914 was purchased by the St. Joseph-Chicago Steamship Company and placed on the namesake route.

The *Eastland's* stability problem was increased as a direct result of the April 1912 loss of the *Titanic*. The loudest "hue and cry" from the tragedy was the bellow of, "lifeboats for all," the crazy notion that every passenger needed a seat in a lifeboat. The fact was however, that until the *Titanic* loss no passenger liner that sank ever needed to lower all of her boats into the water. No passenger vessel ever sank requiring passengers and crew to bob around in lifeboats waiting rescue! Invariably other vessels arrived on the scene before the liner sank and rescued the passengers and crew.

The Eastland *was known to be "tender." Stonehouse Collection*

To comply with the heavy handed government regulation, the *Eastland* added lifeboats to her upper deck (the only place they would fit), adding to her stability problem. Patching a rotted upper deck with tons of concrete made a notoriously tender ship more so. On July 24, 1915 the Western Electric Company's Hawthorne Club, named for the factory in Cicero, Illinois, sponsored an employee picnic to Michigan City, Indiana. To get to there, six vessels, including the infamous *Eastland* were chartered.

There was a strong perception among the employees that attendance at the cruise was a "command performance." If you did not go, your job was at risk. Employees were urged to bring wives, husbands, girlfriends and just plain friends. It was to be a great day and everyone was welcome. Since tickets were only 75 cents, it was a cheap trip.

On the big day all six vessels were moored in the Chicago River waiting for the holiday makers to load. By a little after 7:00 a.m. the *Eastland* reached her licensed capacity of 2,500 passengers. There is some question of the exact sequence of events and what may have triggered the disaster, but at 7:20 a.m. the steamer slowly rolled over on her portside.[xxviii]

The tales of the women aboard range from tragic to lucky. All illustrate how quickly disaster can strike and the thin bonds that bind our lives to earth broken.

While each of the approximately 2,500 souls aboard the *Eastland* has a story, I feel the following, focusing on the women passengers, perhaps best illustrate the tragedy of the disaster.

The experience of Elizabeth Olinger and her husband was a case in point. Both were eventually dragged out alive from inside the ship after she rolled in the river. Although they were rescued together, it was the husband that was interviewed, certainly an interesting commentary on the times. "We just walked up the main deck and were about to sit down when the boat began to list. The people paid little attention to it at first, but after it rolled from side to side several times the boys and girls began to laugh and make fun of it. When it would go over first on one side and then the other they would laugh and shout altogether, hey."

"Then the boat began to lean toward the river and slowly rolled over. I grabbed Elizabeth and we both scrambled toward the upper side. We clung there to a post or brace and looking down we could see the water pouring in below us like falls. It rushed along by the stairs and spurted through cracks and portholes. Men and women were floundering around and screaming as the water rose. In the place where we were there were about twenty women and seven men. The men helped the women to places where they could cling until help arrived, but many sank during the first five minutes and did not come up."

"I kissed Elizabeth and we made preparations to die. I am not a church member but I prayed aloud. Some of the women became hysterical. Others were stoically calm, clinging to the side of the boat and shivering in their wet clothes. As the minutes passed we knew that we were resting on the river bottom and had a chance. Then came the tramping of feet above on the hull. Portholes were opened and the voices of policemen and firemen came to us."

"My wife feared the police would try to pull her through a porthole and she was afraid her dress would be ruined. She took off her wet skirt and rolled it up and I put it in my pocket. During our wait we witnessed many such funny moments. One woman threw her pocket book and all her belongings into the water but clung to her umbrella. She had it when she was pulled out."

"When they were cutting through (the steel hull) with acetylene torches the hot steel was blown all over us and some of the women who had remained calm up to that time began to shriek. Some of them were burned slightly but I think all who had stayed above the water after the first plunge were saved."[xxix]

J. Peterson and his wife Jenny and her sister Miss Mabel Gunderson were on the second deck next to the riverside (the side that ended up river down) when the *Eastland* rolled. They survived in a remarkable escape, washing completely through the ship when an internal partition gave way. Her husband remembered, "We were standing near the rail a little toward the forward of the boat. I could see down either into the engine room or the bar room. The first thing I heard was something that sounded like beer cases falling

The Eastland on her portside. Note the victims standing on her hull and the number of rescue boats. Stonehouse Collection

over. I dropped my cane and it went slipping across the deck toward the cabin. I leaned over to reach for it, but before I could grab it I was kicking about in the water.

"I can swim and I rose with the water. The partition above me gave way. At least some of the windows (unidentified) and I went up through the cabin. I caught hold of a long beam supporting the upper deck, with some others. This beam gave way though, and I had to swim again."

"One man who was hanging on with only his nose, eyes and mouth out of water disappeared when the beam broke and I didn't see him again. The water rose some more and I leaped and caught another two by four. I saw women and men all come up around me and a lot of them went down again. There were about 20 near me who were saved."

"While I was hanging there my wife came up right where I had. She had her hat and coat on and was holding a dollar bill in one hand. I helped her to hold on to a piece of wood and said, "Now hold on there Jenny and don't move.""

"Just then Mabel came up where my wife had appeared. I don't see how either one of them was saved for neither can swim. The strange part of it was that when Mabel came up she had on a life preserver strapped about her body. She said she had found it floating near her and had asked a girl to tie it on her. Just as the girl was doing this, Mabel said, she slid off into the water and was gone. Jenny and Mabel evidently had been carried up by the swirl of the water through the same break in the partition I had passed through.

"When the police came we were about ten feet below the wire screen on the upper side.

"They let ropes down and pulled Jenny and Mabel up. I helped the police draw up the women. There was an excited man who told me his wife had been saved and pleaded to be allowed to go up next. I saw a woman holding a baby in her arms and I snatched the rope from him. I gave it to the woman and told her how to fasten it. She was pulled up still holding the baby."[xxx]

As expected following the disaster, people remembered all sorts of premonitions. One involved a young married couple. The

An unidentified female victim is recovered by a diver. Stonehouse Collection

couple's landlady, Mrs. Paul Altman recalled that, "both had a dread of the boat. Now both are dead. They were so happy Friday night when Mrs. Janke was fussing over the lunch (picnic lunch to be carried on the boat) she stopped and expressed a fear that something would happen to the boat. Later Mr. Janke rang my bell. Here is my key and $50 for my mother if we don't come back from the trip he said. I still have the key. Their relatives came this morning and opened the flat. They found a letter on the dresser and also a will. Mrs. Janke wished that her mother might have her bracelet and rings and I gave them the money."[xxxi]

Young Josie Markowska, age 18, also was said to have a premonition, at least according to her friend Helen Glinka who claimed, "Josie told my mother she felt something awful was going to happen and that she did not want to go to the picnic. My mother laughingly told her to go on and have a good time and warned her not to think of disaster else she might bring it on the boat. Now she is dead."[xxxii]

Women were involved in ways other than being victims. Many of the dead were brought to the local armory as a temporary morgue. At one point it was claimed 500 people looking for loved ones were in the hall. When women with little children came by to identify loved ones, other women acted as baby sitters to spare the children the horror of seeing the hundreds of bodies laid out on the cold floor. Three other women, Miss Elizabeth Todhunter, Mrs.

The bodies of victims were laid out in temporary morgues for identification. Stonehouse Collection

C.E. Dunn and Mrs. Edgar McGraw, handed bottles of ice water to those waiting in line to identify victims. The *Chicago Tribune* estimated more than 150 women required medical support as the result of becoming hysterical with the waiting or fainting from the stress. Nurses on hand later claimed only two of the 150 were actually relatives searching for victims. The rest were simply the curious exploring at the hall strictly out of a sense of morbid curiosity.[xxxiii]

The Women's Trade Union League, a Chicago based labor organization quickly accused the *Eastland's* owners of "criminal greed" as the root cause of the disaster. They also called for a full investigation and to prosecute those held responsible.

There were also instances in which people thought dead, returned unexpectedly to their families. There was jubilation in the home of the Glinka sisters when Anna walked in with a tale of survival, but she was the only one of a group of four friends to live through the disaster. She said, "I was clinging to the deck like a fly. (*Eastland* was now on her side and the deck was near vertical). One of the girls was holding on to each of my feet and the third to an arm. Just when I could hold no longer their hands slipped from me and I heard them go down with a splash. A man tried to push me off and while I was pleading with him two other men reached down and dragged me up on the slippery side of the boat. Sitting on the edge, they passed me across their legs to a lifeboat."[xxxiv]

Her husband, lying on his stomach across the hull, pulled Mrs. Paul Krones to safety. Her tight skirt made it impossible for her to swing her foot up to get a purchase. Only when another man managed to grab her foot was her husband able to drag her to safety. Since there were five children at home, her death would have been especially devastating.[xxxv]

Another man heroically managed to save his entire party, including wife, mother, daughter, brother and girlfriend. In addition, his wife hauled three little girls to safety. She later recalled, "I lifted up a sturdy blond boy of 4 and a dark haired girl of 7. There was another little girl of 9 years old and a tot of 3. My husband must have helped save 50. A women in a black satin dress who said her husband, whom she married in June, had been drowned, fought against being saved. We dragged her out against her will. Another woman whom we pulled out said her husband and 5 children had gone down. One fat woman became wedged in a porthole and her shoulders were badly cut and torn before we got her out. One sight I shall never forget is a woman holding her baby above the water. The baby was calmly sucking a rubber nipple. Both mother and child sank before we could reach them.[xxxvi]

Mrs. Albert Pearson remembered, "I was sitting on the side near the pier. My husband had just gone with some friends into the smoking room. Suddenly the boat began to sway and then it turned over on its side. I hung onto a rail and was pulled out of a window onto the upper side of the boat. I have not seen my husband but I am afraid he is lost." Mrs. Pearson received a deep cut on her arm when she was pulled through the window.[xxxvii]

"Women and children first" may have been the cry on the *Titanic* but not on the *Eastland* where it was every man, woman and child for themselves. Joe Lannon, the fountain man on the lower deck remembered when the ship started to roll everyone took it as a joke. The dance floor was crowded with women and soon they were sliding madly across the floor. Panic reigned. He reported seeing men tear women and girls away from where they were clinging to rails above the water so they could take their places. Chivalry was non-existent. Stronger men pulled weaker women from safe perches forcing them into the water where they drowned in a gurgle of bubbles. Lannon and another fountain man made it to the outside of the hull and back to one of the portholes into the dance floor deck where they pulled others through to safety. He remembered one of the girls they hauled through the narrow hole fainted immediately on reaching the outside. In another instance the woman they were pulling through was so heavy they could barely pick her up. After a struggle, she finally "popped" through the hole.[xxxviii]

There were incredible scenes of personal tragedy. It was reported city Fireman Fred Swigert spent three hours lifting bodies from the ship when a diver handed him the remains of a little girl. He placed the body on a stretcher and looked closely at it. After a second a

The Chicago newspapers covered the disaster in excruciating detail.
Stonehouse Collection

look of recognition flashed across his face and he collapsed! She was his daughter! Another city worker had a similar experience. Louis Schleiert, an employee of the Fire Prevention Bureau was working frantically with a torch and axe to cut his way inside the hull. He knew his wife and two children were in the wreck... somewhere. Working and swimming through the flooded and wrecked cabins, he made his way deep into the dead ship where he discovered the lifeless bodies of all three locked together in death. He collapsed with shock, and was rushed to the hospital unconscious by other firemen.[xxxix]

Lillian Heideman remembered, "I was one of the last to get aboard. With me were Anna Tempanski, Elsie Reinhardt and Margaret Tomshen. We had just checked our lunches and were in the washroom on the middle deck when the ship started to lean over. We became frightened and ran up to the upper deck where we found that the boat was leaning way over. The girls with me began to scream as the water came up about their ankles and the next thing I knew we were all struggling in the water. I went down and down. Water rushed into my mouth and nose. Then I came up. A man pushed a plank in my direction. I reached for it; it slipped from my grasp and down I went again. I came up again and another man threw me a rope. Somehow I managed to get the rope around me and I was pulled free.[xl]

Policeman John Poot arrived at the wreck as soon as the alarm was given. The entire scene was chaotic. People were everywhere and the pitiful cries for help echoing on the river. Finding a boat without oars, he jumped in and paddled to the wreck using his hands as oars. On the way he hauled aboard a child and three men holding on to a piece of floating wreckage. A woman drowned before he could reach her. On the wreck he and one of the men pulled three women out of the hull through portholes a bare 18 inches wide. When he looked down the slender hole to see if there were others still inside he saw a woman clinging to a beam and dropped her a rope. The woman held tight to the rope as Poot and his companions tried to pull her through the hole, but she was too fat and couldn't squeeze through. Poot tried to find a cutting torch to widen the hole, but the woman gave up and sank beneath the waves.[xli]

As firemen cut their way into the wreck, more and more victims were found. Many were dead but a lucky few were alive. When they cut into a stateroom the men were happy to find two women still living but reportedly both were driven mad by the horror of being trapped in the dead ship.[xlii]

The *Material Service* Bombing

Women working the lakes not only faced dangers from storm and shipwreck but also from crime. A case in point is the strange bombing on the motor vessel *Material Service*. The 240-foot long motorized barge was built in Sturgeon Bay, Wisconsin by the Smith Dock Company and launched in 1929. Only 14-1/2 feet in height, she was designed to pass under the many bridges around Chicago while hauling gravel and sand to various construction sites. To facilitate material handling, she had eight 30 by 10-foot cargo holds with a 90-foot conveyor belt self-unloading system.

On November 30, 1930 the *Material Service* was moving through the Chicago Sanitary and Ship Canal when a powerful explosion, centered in the engine room, rocked the ship. Its force blew into the crew's quarters, galley and pilothouse, injuring seven of the crew, including the female cook who would later die from her wounds. Subsequent investigation concluded the blast had nothing to do with the ship's machinery, but rather was caused by a bomb placed by person or persons unknown. The culprits were never identified but it is easy to speculate based on the wide spread corruption in the Chicago political scene; it was intended to be either a warning or retribution. Whatever it was, the act left a woman dead.

The *Material Service* continued her gravel filled life until July 29, 1936. Running on Lake Michigan just short of the South Chicago Light she suddenly capsized drowning 15 of the 22 men aboard. The lake was choppy and water entered the holds through her open hatches. By the time the crew realized the danger it was too late.[xliii]

The barge Material Service *was an important part of the Chicago maritime scene.* Stonehouse Collection

CHAPTER THREE

THE CHRISTMAS GIFTS OF THE WAVES

The following item from the *Oswego Times and Journal* of January 30, 1856 well illustrates the horror of both shipwreck and difficulty of life for family members trying to carry on. It was as difficult then as it is now. The story is fictional but none-the-less, does represent the fate of many shipwrecks on the lakes.

"Wind closed in upon a stormy November day. As the sun set the wind had lulled, though the great waves still beat upon the rocky shore. They broke violently over the massive stone piers and curled over the tower, dashing against the thick panes thro' which the kindly lamp shown out to indicate a port to storm tossed mariners; or as was sometimes the case, to keep the craft of provident captains with closely reefed sails lying to outside until daylight shone upon the shore.

"Overhead the sky, with the twilight assumed a uniform grey, almost black, tint; but along the line of the horizon, where the arch dipped into the great plain of water, a lurid streak appeared, which lighted up the wild scene. As far as the eye could see, the waves were tossing tumultuously, their white crests relieved against the fiery brightness of the horizon. In the very central of this line of light slowly uprose the masts and rigging, and then the dark hull of a vessel, every shroud and sheet and yard clearly defined as it stood out, black and distinct against the flame colored background.

"The man from the lighthouse saw it and so did some other watchers, perhaps relatives of men who were known to be on board vessels bound downward, during this fearful storm, which had already ranted two days. Anxiety and thought of the danger of those who were at the mercy of the elements had drawn some forth, in spite of the storm, to watch for approaching vessels. These men, wise in weather-signs, shook their heads ominously as they saw this vessel lying there, and looking like a picture drawn in ink against the red sky–a dark "phantom ship." And they said to each other, that the captain would never venture to enter that dangerous port until morning, for the wind blew hard on shore, and the bar which stretched across the river's mouth was almost bare, except in the deepest part of the channel. But they watched still until the night fell, and the light fading out of the horizon, sky and water and land were all shrouded in the inky blackness of the wild, stormy night.

"There was, as one might well believe, great anxiety and wakefulness in sailor's homes. Many a wife sat helplessly with her helpless children beside the fireside, and thought of her absent husband and father. Many tearful prayers went up, and many a lonely pillow was wet with tears, called forth by shuddering fear and impotent anxiety. Danger is harder to be borne by those who sit powerlessly at home, than by those who meet it face to face. Those who mourn by the fireside, could they once feel the power to aid and save, would rush to the rescue, of the peril of life and limb, strong and confident, and even hopeful.

"We talk, we write, we think of the perils of those who go forth to the battlefield, but to them comes courage in the direct emergency, and in the greatest danger, home whispers of deliverance. It is upon the helpless ones at home that wearying care and the sickness of "hope deferred" falls most heavily.

"Anna Henderson was the wife of a lake captain. Her house stood upon the hillside and from its windows she could see the port and the wide expanse of waters, and on a clear day, could even trace the faint blue line, near the horizon, which she had been to, was the shore of Canada. The very morning of which the gale commenced she had received a letter from her husband as he was about leaving his port upon an upper lake, for home: and how she was anxiously looking for his vessel. All day long she had watched the dreary waters, and as night fell had seen the vessel that loomed in relief against the lurid sky. By the aid of a glass she could distinctly see that it was a three masted vessel, like that of which her husband commanded. Beyond that she could discern nothing. Very soon the light faded and when the thick darkness shut out every object, she closed the curtains and sat down, with her little ones, to wait. The children had heard that papa was coming home, and their merry prattle fell almost painfully upon her anxious ear. But the lesson of patience had too often coned, and she sat gently as if every nerve were not strained to listen for the footfall she loved to hear—quietly as if her sprit were not wandering afar over the dreary waste of waters, in search of the expected one, in his danger and suffering.

"And thus she sat long after her children were dreaming the placid dream of infancy in their little crib. At midnight, the wind which had temporarily lulled, sprang up again; and as if made furious by its short quietude, howled and roared along the bleak hillside as though a thousand demons were riding upon its pinions. The waves too, which had fallen with a solemn cadence upon the shore, now roared and surged as if lashed to fury and Anna could hear them as they beat upon the beach with thundering noise. Oh! How she trembled at every sound! The shrieking mariners, and every wave beat to tell of the destruction of the frail timbers which alone divided her husband and his sturdy crew from a grave in the foaming waters.

"Thus she passed the night; and the first faint rays of dawn, stealing through her window, fell upon her kneeling figure as beside the bed where her children slept she prayed for him whom she thought struggling with the fury of the storm.

"On board the vessel, which had as suddenly appeared in relief against the red sky, were twelve men—a large crew for a lake vessel—but this was of extraordinary size. James Henderson, its captain, well wrapped in waterproof clothing, and with his sou'wester upon his head, stood upon the deck, over which the waves rolled continuously, as the vessel dipped into the troughs of the sea. His uncouth garments did not hide the muscular proportions of his figure, and there was an expression of dauntless courage on the handsome, though weather browned face, which told that, though he knew the danger, he did not fear it.

"The crew, similarly dressed, were standing in different attitudes around, holding by the bulwarks and rigging for the force of the waves was great. But few of them had sought the protection of the cabin, though, with the exception of the man at the helm, not one of them had any employment. They were all watchful and anxious, but confident and hopeful. They had caught the first faint glimmer of the lighthouse lamps, and knew that their port and homes were in sight, but only to be reached through much peril: for the harbor of Oswego, which they approached is an artificial one, formed by two massive piers which extend nearly half way across the mouth of the river, from each shore. The narrow entrance between these piers is always dangerous in stormy weather, though a safe port is found within where a navy might ride in security.

"As the darkness settled down, the vessel sped on with only enough sail to keep her to her course. The far shining light guided her onward and it was the unanimous voice of the men, that an entrance should be attempted, and although the captain thought otherwise, he felt that the perils of entering the harbor or laying to outside in this fearful storm were about equally balanced; and he listened to the advice of some of his veteran sailors who had seen twice as many years as himself. He apprehended a rising of the wind at midnight, but hoped to reach port before that hour.

"On then struggled the noble craft but her progress was slow. The wind rose as she stood off and on, striving to effect an entrance to the harbor. As if maddened by the fury of the assault, she plunged into the huge waves, which rolled off her decks, and would have swept every man into the boiling surges but that they had lashed themselves to the rigging. The entrance was very near; the light from the beacon lamps fell upon their stern, anxious faces. A few moments more, and they would have been safe; but yielding to the fury of the wind, the vessel shot past the narrow opening, and in a moment, with a shock and crash which sent one mast, with it's rigging and the men lashed to it, overboard, she struck upon the pier. Again she recedes, and again with a heavier crash, her bow runs far up the pier; another mast topples and with its living freight, is swept away. Another crash, and the heavy timbers quiver and part in the center. Two or three men cling to the forward part of the vessel; the rest are swept away, and the cries of their despair are soon smothered in the boiling waves.

"Over those who remain, the waves break every instant. It is intensely cold, and soon they are covered with ice, and their numbed hands and powerless limbs relax their grasp, and all but one are carried away into the darkness and heavy sea. He is lashed to the bulwark and although insensible, is not borne away. Thus in sight of their homes, and with the rays of the beacon which they fondly hoped would light them to safety, they one by one, go down to their watery grave.

"The morning dawned upon this sad spectacle. With much danger and difficulty the sole survivor was saved; and borne to his home, the only one where those twelve men had dwelt which had not, that day, to mourn his death. Ann Henderson had not risen from her prayerful vigil by the beside of her children when she learned that she was a widow and they fatherless.

"We draw a veil over the scenes which followed in that bereaved household. The little children wailed their infantile grief away but the agony of such desolation as fell upon the widow's heart has no voice nor speech. In her sorrow she moved about the home–his no longer. For hours she would stand and gaze out upon the busy port, and the broad lake which smiled treacherous calm in the sunlight of the pleasant days which followed that fearful storm amidst which its waves engulfed her young husband. Alas, how often she pictured to herself every event of that awful night.

"The inky blackness which shrouded the horror of the wreck when the waves swallowed up those living forms, and the dim beacon rays gleamed back from their crests and the ice covered shrouds of the lost vessel. There was a dull heavy despair in her heart, which shut out all sense of present duties and brooded silently over the memory of the lost. There was but one strong feeling in her soul, and that was that the waves might give up the body of her husband, that she might look once more upon his face, and see him laid to rest beside her father and his mother in the burial ground.

"Thus slowly the days and weeks passed on and Christmas Eve had come. The children, who had prattled all day of Santa Claus and his expected gifts, had gone to rest, at length, and the widow sat alone by her fireside. Opposite her was placed the chair where one year ago, her husband had sat in his proud strength. He had come home with pockets filled with Christmas gifts for the little ones and together they had taken down the tiny stockings which the chubby little hands had suspended, and had filled them to overflowing with toys and all manner of good things, talking all the while of their darlings whose delight upon the morrow they smiling played, as fond parents will. She remembered his smile and his kiss as he presented to her the handsome dress now hanging all unused–and never to be worn again–and she glanced down at her mourning robes, and with deeper sighs thought of him for whom she wore them, sleeping afar in his watery grave.

"It is only to unbroken households that perfect joy comes with the holiday time. There are too many memories of the loved and lost clustering about those days of wonted festivity, to allow them to be otherwise than very sad days to those whom death has robbed of the friends whose smiles brightened those once joyous anniversaries. Treasured words, and looks and acts of kindness rise up, then from the depths of memory; and the desolation of our longing hearts grows sometimes almost too intense for endurance.

"The wind was blowing fresh and the widow could hear the solemn beat of the waves upon the shore. They seemed to sound the requiem of him who rested in their depths, and their voice was mournful as were the thoughts which filled her soul–straining her ear she listened till her heart seemed bursting. Her husband's voice seemed calling to her in every sigh of the wind, and she must go forth to meet him. Hastily wrapping herself in a large cloak, she sallied forth into the darkness of the night.

"It was late here she returned, drenched and weary, and sought her lonely couch. She had been wandering up and down the beach, and straining her gaze for she knew not what, but all the while full of that wild hope that the wave might cast the body of her husband at her feet. It was only when utterly exhausted that she sought her home. For the first time in all those sad weeks, she slept soundly for many hours, the sleep of utter weariness.

"She dreamed of her lost husband, a pleasant, happy dream. He walked beside her and her little ones, in some green, quiet spot, and talked of the future of those that had been given to her care; and though he spoke of a far-off journey, it brought no sadness, for the thought of the happy occupation he had pointed out to fill his absence. Happy, and quite lifted out of herself, she seemed to hear the joyous sounds of bells mingling with his words in tones that gave her courage and cheerfulness. She awoke and found that the sound had not died away.

"As she lay calm and happy from her late vision, she had heard the sweet chime from St. Paul's tower, and it seemed to say, "peace, goodwill," "peace, goodwill." The tones filled her soul with the sweetest peace she had ever known, and it was with strength of purpose unknown to her before that she listened. The great bell of St. Mark's took up the exultant strain, its deep tone seeming to swell the chorus in those words of loftiest praise, "Glory to God in the highest." She slept again, and in the morning awoke with a lighter heart that had beat in her bosom since the dismal dawn which first looked upon her great sorrow.

"The clamor of the children for their Christmas gifts, almost overcame her little fortitude as they sat at breakfast. But she showed them her mourning weeds and their sad-colored garments, and bade them ask of their father in heaven such gifts as they most needed, and denied them from an earthly father. A look of awe came over the little, eager faces, at her words, and silence fell upon the group. It was broken by a loud knock at the door, which brought all to their feet. A pleasant voice was heard parleying with the servant in the entry, for a moment, then the inner door opened and Anna found herself clasped in the warm embrace of her only brother.

"It was a happy meeting, yet saddened by the absence of the hearty welcome of that one whom all missed from the head of his table. Anna felt a great portion of her desolation lifted from her soul, as she heard the cheerful voice and saw the earnest, confident face of her much-loved brother. She was not utterly alone, not all forsaken. She had thought of God in the nighttime, when the sweet bells rand rang out the anthem of the Nativity, and how he had sent this good and noble brother to be her stay and protector.

"They sat in long conversation–sometimes sad and sometimes cheerful. All the sad story of the wreck, and a thousand other incidents which had filled up a long separation were discussed till in the midst came another knock at the outer door. Presently the brother called out, and Anna sat thoughtful but comforted where he left her. The dark midnight of her sorrow had passed, and the dawn of cheerful endurance was brightening her soul.

"Presently her brother returned. He kissed her cheek fondly, and passed his arm about her. He led her trembling with a strange joy, half mournfulness, half delight, into another room. A strange dark object was stretched upon a table there, and in a moment, Anna looked upon the face of her dead husband.

"The waters had given up their dead. Upon the very beach where she had wandered but the last night his body had been cast up, as if in answer to the longing prayer of the bereaved wife. And there he lay almost unchanged, his features rigid, but calm and peaceful, with the firm set lip still expressive of the courage with which he met his fate.

"And Anna Henderson's chief wish was gratified. All that remained of him she loved so had been given back to her. A strong arm, if not the one she loved, was hers to lean upon, and she could show her children the spot where she had laid the mortal remains of one who had perished nobly in the performance of his duty, leaving to him the legacy of an unstained character, and humble thought he had been, a true manhood.

"These were Anna Henderson's Christmas gifts–the body of her lost husband, and the dawning of an earnest purpose in her soul, to live for the duties, the cares and the joys that remained to her in life."[xliv]

CHAPTER FOUR
ON THE BEACH

A Maiden's Lot

Being a woman on the Great Lakes frontier was always difficult. Being an Ojibwe woman perhaps doubly so, especially if selected for a dubious honor.

This tale revolves around the famous Ontonagon Boulder, a massive hunk of "native" or pure copper resting in the Ontonagon River, some ten miles upstream from Lake Superior. Indians mined the Keweenaw copper for 5,000 years and its use for tools and ornaments is legendary. But the Boulder was special. The local Ojibwe considered it a shrine. It was their "Manitou," or mediator between the tribe and the gods. Early stories described it as being as big as a house although such tales were more imagination than fact.

The first Europeans to see the boulder were the French voyageurs who cut off souvenirs for King Louis XIV as early as 1665. A century later English fur trader Alexander Henry was shown the boulder by the local Ojibwe. Indian agent Henry Rowe Schoolcraft measured it as 3-foot, 8-inches by 3-foot, 4-inches.

In 1843 James K. Paul, a resident of the lead mining district of Wisconsin, decided he had to have the massive boulder. Guided by a little Indian girl, he and a companion located the stone and with great effort he managed to haul it to Ontonagon aboard a bateau.[xlv] After being exhibited in Detroit as a sideshow curiosity, it was seized by the U.S. government and taken to Washington as a unique mineral

This old wood cut shows a group of early explorers (note the flags at the sterns of the last two canoes), making their way to the famous copper boulder. Stonehouse Collection

specimen. Eventually the boulder ended up in the Smithsonian Institution in Washington, DC.[xlvi] Paul took the $1,362 the government paid him in compensation and opened the Deadfall Saloon at the mouth of the Ontonagon River, thus founding the village of Ontonagon. By this time the weight of the boulder was reduced to 3,708 pounds, considerably less than original estimated five tons before nearly 200 years of tourists hacked pieces off as mementoes.[xlvii]

There are numerous Ojibwe legends concerning the boulder. It was said, they often covered it in the smoke of a calumet (pipe) and it spoke to them in a "voice of thunder and demanded a human sacrifice;" and in accordance with this belief, they were accustomed, on occasions to immolate at it's shrine a prisoner of war. On one occasion, when an important and hazardous expedition had been resolved upon they sacrificed a beautiful maiden of fifteen years of age who had been taken prisoner in one of their hostile excursions among neighboring tribes."[xlviii]

The Jesuit missionary Charlevoix related the story in a letter to his superior. "After having a lodge appointed for her, attendants to meet her every wish and her neck, arms and ankles covered with bracelets of silver and copper, she was led to believe she was to become the bride of the son of the head chief. The time appointed was the end of the winter and she felt rejoiced as the time rolled on, waiting for the season of her happiness. The day fixed upon for the sacrifice having dawned, she passed through all the preparatory ceremonies and was dressed in her best attire, being covered with all the ornaments the settlement could command, after which she was placed in the midst of a circle of warriors, dressed in their war suits, who seemed to escort her for the purpose of showing their deference. Besides their usual arms, each one carried several pieces of wood, which he had received from the girl. She had carried wood to the rock on the preceding day, which she had helped to gather in the forest. Believing she was to be elevated to high rank, her ideas being of the most pleasing character, the poor girl advanced to the alter with rapturous feelings of joy and timidity, which would be naturally raised in the bosom of a young female of her age. As the procession proceeded, which occupied some time, savage music accompanied them and chants, invoking the intervention of their "Manitou" that the Great Spirit would prosper their enterprise; so that being excited by the music and dancing, the deceitful delusion under which she had been kept remained until the last moment."

"But as soon as she had reached the place of sacrifice, where nothing was to be seen but fires, torches and instruments of torture, her eyes were opened, her fate was revealed to her and she became aware of her terrible destiny, as she had often heard of the mysterious sacrifices of the Copper Rock. What must have been her feelings! How great her surprise! How terrible the change when she no longer had any doubt of their intentions. Who could describe the terrible horror of the moment? Her cries resounded through the forest but neither tears nor entreaties prevailed. She conjured the stern warriors who surrounded her to have pity on her youth and innocence but all in vain, as the Indian priests coolly proceeded with the horrid ceremonies. Nothing could prevail against their superstition and the horrid demands of the copper monster, which called for a human sacrifice. She was tied with withes to the top of the rock. The fire was gradually applied to her with torches made of the wood she had with her own hands distributed to the warriors. When exhausted with her cries and about expiring, her tormentors opened the circle that had surrounded her and the great chief shot an arrow into her heart, which was followed by the spears and arrows of his followers and the blood poured down the sides of the glistening rock in streams."[xlix]

Whether the story is true or not is unknown. The Jesuit related what he had been told, not what he personally saw.

According to legend, an Indian woman was also the reason for the naming of the Ontonagon River. Ontonagon (Nantaonagon) is derived from the Ojibwe language meaning "lost bowl." Supposedly a young Ojibwe girl was washing dishes at the mouth of the river when a bowl swept away in the current, thus giving the river it's name.[1]

The Minesota mine (the spelling is the result of a filing error), was an immensely rich producer of copper. Stonehouse Collection

The Ontonagon area did have a short run as a major copper producer. At the height of the boom 6,000 people lived in village while the Minnesota Mine[li] paid out millions of dollars in dividends. Some of the chunks of copper discovered in area were huge. One "piece" discovered in the Minnesota Mine measured *12-1/2 feet by 18-1/2 feet by 46-feet, with an estimated weight of 527 tons!* It took a crew of 20 men 15 months to chisel it down to chunks small enough to hoist out of the mine. This hunk was 285 times larger than the famous Ontonagon Boulder.[lii] Finding large pieces of mass copper was rarely a good thing. They were very difficult and time consuming to move or break into smaller pieces. It was always better to find many small hunks than one big one. Regardless of size, by the 1880s, copper mining in the area was finished.

The Last Battle

There is a little known tale concerning the last battle the Keweenaw Ojibwe fought that is illustrative of the important role that Indian women sometimes played on the periphery of events.

The following account was gathered and written by the Reverend Edward Jacker and later forwarded to the Houghton County Historical Society in the 1890s.

"Sailing up from the mouth of Portage River, at a distance of about two and a half miles, you pass a large wood dock (Church's) then, turning with the river, you perceive to the left a slightly wooded point, partly cut off by a bayou, but connected with the main land by a low, marshy ground, which at the time of the event, may possibly have formed a branch of the channel; this is Battle Island, a rather incorrect translation of the Indian 'Tchibai Minis' (pronounced Che-bae-ee-me-niss), that is, the Island of the Dead.

"The generations have passed since the last battle fought between the Otchipwe (Ojibwe) and Iroquois Indians took place. The point of land at the south of the Portage River, now disconnected from the main land by the Ship Canal, was at that time, as it continued to be until the beginning of the present century, the site of a large Otchipwe village. One day it happened that a young man started from this place toward the point now occupied by the lighthouse, to pay a visit to a young woman, his intended wife; when at once he descried, in the direction of Traverse Island, something like two large logs floating on the surface of the lake. A closer examination revealed to him the startling fact that the objects seen were nothing less than two large Iroquois canoes, apparently manned by a strong war party. The young brave kept himself concealed until he was satisfied that the enemy had landed at the beach next to the lighthouse point, from whence they undoubtedly would soon wind their way through the woods and bushes, to surprise in the darkness of night and massacre the inhabitants of the Otchipwe village. Hurrying back thither, he communicated the strange news, whereupon a plan of escape as well as retaliation was instantly settled. All the domestic animals–only dogs of course–were killed, to prevent their betraying by their barking, the intended general move. Then the whole population embarked in their canoes and took to the river. The females and children were sent as far as Torch Lake as a place of safety in the case of untoward events; the warriors concealed themselves and their canoes on both shores of the river, on and opposite the point, which was to obtain its name from the following stroke of Indian strategy.

"It was not long before the waylaying party received the news of the Iroquois approach, for two young heroes, mere boys, had been left behind, concealed in the bushes across the river's mouth, to watch the movements of the enemy.

"The Iroquois (Nadowey) at their arrival, finding the village deserted, the dogs slain, wigwams empty, broke out into a terrific howl, with mingled expressions of rage and disappointment. Upon this, the boys let fly among them some arrows, which coming from unseen quarters, served to increase their bewilderment and probably filled their minds with superstitious misgivings. They seemed to hold a consultation, at the end of which they took to their canoes, in pursuit of the Otchipwes, but were outrun by the little reconnoitering party, who brought the welcome news to the waylaying Indians at Battle Island, just in time to have them prepared for action.

"It was night, but the two long canoes were soon plainly seen in hot pursuit, paddled along by many strong arms through the middle of the channel. A shower of sharp-pointed arrows met the foe, striking some, discouraging the rest. The Iroquois neared the opposite shore, to meet another cloud of missiles; their ranks were quickly thinned, and soon the boats were seen motionless floating on the bloodstained water. Every invader had been slain, but one young boy, who was found alive and unhurt in the bottom of a canoe; and he was weeping. 'We shall not hurt you, child' the victorious band said; 'Go home in peace, and bid the men of the tribe come up and pay a visit to the Otchipwe country; we warrant them a hearty welcome.' Upon which he only wept more and said: 'Alas, there are no more Iroquois left but women and children.' In pity, they sent him off with a badge of safe conduct; and it is believed he reached his native village somewhere on the lower lakes.

"This is the history of the fight, or rather the massacre of Battle Island, as preserved in the memory of the Keweenaw Indians. Will it be worth the while to make an attempt at critical examination of the facts contained in this simple narrative? If so, the first question will be, on whose authority do these facts rest? And here the precedence must be given to the fair sex.

"Nibinckwadokwe, pronounced Ne-be-na-quah-duck-wa, that is, 'the woman of the clouds standing in a bow,' is a person of clear intellect and undoubted veracity; she enjoys a remarkably attentive memory, especially for one of her age, which is about seventy. This good woman, when a child of probably ten years, heard the story of the massacre repeated by an eye-witness of the scene–her own grandfather–Ojinini, pronounced Oh-zhe-ne-ne, 'the handsome man,' one of the mere boys who sent their arrows across the mouth of the Portage River among the Iroquois raiders and afterward a noted chief of the Portage Lake band of Indians, she remembers perfectly well, as an old man, probably a nonagenarian, if not more, who used to grope his way along the net poles, from lodge to lodge, in her native village at the mouth of the Pilgrim River. The remembrance of his words was, of course, kept fresh in her mind by their frequent repetition in the family wigwam; and the story, as rendered by her, coincides almost in every particular with the account given of the same event by other persons of her age, who probably have it from a different source. Its intrinsic evidence of truth also leaves scarcely anything to be desired. The accuracy of the statement, together with those seemingly trifling incidents, which could scarcely have been invented by narrators of a later day, such as the visit of the lover, the dogs, etc., give to the whole story an air of truthfulness, which vouches for the general correctness of the relation.

"The assertion of the young Iroquois captive, that there were none but widows and orphans left of his tribe, which literally interpreted, would of course, imply a great exaggeration, may have been true too, in this sense, that all the warriors of one particular band had participated in the ill-starred campaign. And in fact, this encounter between the two hostile nations, on Otchipwe ground, is the last recorded.

"As for the precise year of the event, it is impossible to make out the year, the Indians being rather deficient in chronology, even as far as their own ages are concerned; but by deducting fourteen, the probable age of the young spy Ojiminini, from ninety, which may have been his age at the time of his death, and deducting again the number seventy-six thus gained, from 1806, when his granddaughter Nibinckwadokwe was about ten years old, the year 1730 will be found; and this cannot be far from the true date.

"Traveler or excursionists, if you wish to shake hands with the courageous young spy's granddaughter, stop the course of your boat at the first house that greets you from the river's left shore, after you pass, on your way downward, the second wood dock (Drapeau's) about a mile below Battle Island."[liii]

In this single story weaves the involvement of women in the roles of the lover during the discovery of the Iroquois sneak attack, fleeing with the children and infirm from the Otchipwe camp, "picking up the pieces' after the massacre of the warriors and finally as the story teller relating the event generations later!

Starvation on the Island

The presence of copper on the Keweenaw Peninsula and Isle Royale was known for thousands of years. Early explorers and voyageurs found it in small quantities as well as noticing the Native Americans commonly used copper implements and devices. But it wasn't until Michigan State Geologist Douglass Houghton discovered it in large commercial quantities and detailed the potential in his 1841 report that serious exploitation was considered. A few prospectors arrived on the Keweenaw in 1841 and more in 1842. After Congress signed a treaty with the local Ojibwe in 1843 establishing ownership of much of the area, it was "Katy, bar the door" and the nation's first great mineral rush began! The Keweenaw and Isle Royale too, although to a lesser extent, were overrun with hordes of "prospectors" looking to make their fortune in copper.[liv] While the one-man outfits usually failed, the corporate men were successful and eventually the Michigan mines would produce over 14 billion pounds of copper.

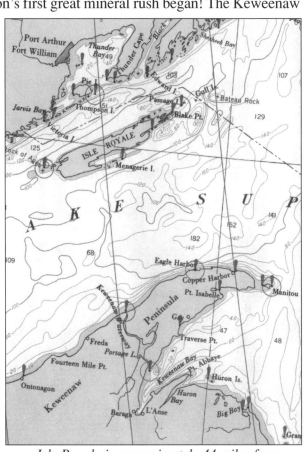

This particular story involves copper mining on Isle Royale, Lake Superior.

Isle Royale is approximately 44 miles from the Keweenaw Peninsula. Stonehouse Collection

Much of the copper was "native" or mass copper, essentially pure metal as opposed to a sulfide ore requiring extensive refining. Native copper could be pried from fissures in the ground and smelted or beat directly into useful objects. In some instances glaciers tore the copper from the rock leaving it loose on the ground. This was often called "float" copper. Copper was also found as lodes in amygdaloidal lava flow tops and conglomerate beds, both requiring considerable effort to extract. Isle Royale, an island approximately 45 miles long and 7 wide, lay 40 miles or so northwest of the Keweenaw, was also found to have significant copper deposits.

The European discovery of copper on Isle Royale as well as the Keweenaw was a bit late. Historians determined that Native Americans had been working the copper for 5,000 years! On Isle Royale alone there were an estimated 1,000 pits attributed to the early Native American miners and copper artifacts were used throughout the Midwest. Copper mining was essentially a boom or bust proposition and there were three cycles of European mining activity on the island. The first period running 1843-1855, second 1873-1881 and third 1889-1893.[iv]

Although the island had long been generally explored and used by both Native Americans and Europeans, it was not a place where people remained for any length of time. Seasonal fishermen worked the island waters from the spring through the early summer, but no one remained over the winter. It was too inhospitable and dangerous a location.

Charlie and Angelique Mott were hired to protect the interests of one of the early copper companies while it organized, filed the proper claim paperwork, etc. In the early days of exploration, Isle Royale was considered a very "hot" area for copper. By 1847 a dozen companies had "prospects" on the island. Charlie and Angelique were truly "accidental tourists."

Angelique was said to be the daughter of Shawano, an Ojibwe chief from Sault Ste. Marie. She was not a frail or petite woman but rather tall and robust. She was also a woman who could "take care of herself."

An idealized sketch of Angelique Mott. Stonehouse Collection

Angelique married Charlie Mott (likely a corruption of La Motte), a French-Canadian voyageur in 1845 and the couple moved to La Pointe on Madeline Island, the largest of the Apostle Islands.[lvi] A Jesuit mission was on the island since 1665 and doubtless Angelique became part of the community.

A poet once described an island as a ship that didn't move. Certainly this is an apt description. Confined in an area with only the resources "aboard" can create considerable problems, especially if there aren't enough resources.

The tale of Charlie and Angelique Mott is a case in point. Like many stories, there are different versions varying in their political correctness. One historian estimated there were 11 different variations. What follows is the one Angelique is credited as writing.

"When I and my husband Charlie Mott were first married we lived at LaPointe. Mr. Douglas, Mr. Bennett and some other "big bugs" from Detroit had come up there in the schooner *Algonquin* looking for copper. From La Pointe, Charlie and I went over with them, on their invitation, to Isle Royale. After landing with the rest,

Madeline Island circa 1840, when Charlie and Angelique lived there.
Stonehouse Collection

I wandered a long way on the beach until I saw something shinning in the water. It was a piece of mass copper. When I told the *Algonquin* people of it they were very glad and determined at once to locate it. They said if Charlie and I would occupy it for them, Charlie should have $25 a month and I $5 a month to cook for him. Having agreed to the bargain, we returned to the Sault to lay in a good supply of provisions. There I first met Mendenhall, the man who brought us into all this trouble. He said there was no need of carrying provisions so far up the lake and at so heavy an expense, as he had plenty of provisions at La Pointe. When we got to La Pointe we found that this was not so. All we could get was a half-barrel of flour (which we had to borrow from the mission), six pounds of butter that smelled bad and was white like lard and a few beans. I didn't want to go to the island until we had something more to live on and I told Charlie so, but Mendenhall over persuaded him. He solemnly promised him two things; First that he would send a bateau[lvii] with provisions in a few weeks; and then, at the end of three months he would be sure to come himself and take us away. So, very much against my will, we went to Isle Royale on the first of July. Having a bark canoe and a net for a while we lived on fish, but one day about the end of summer a storm came and we lost our canoe; and soon our net was broken and good for nothing also. Oh, how we watched and watched and watched but no bateau ever came to supply us with food; no vessel ever came to take us away; neither Mendenhall's nor any other. When at last we found that we had been deserted and that we would have to spend the whole winter on the island and that there would be no getting away until spring, I tell you such a thought was hard to bare indeed. Our flour and butter and beans were gone. We couldn't catch any more fish. Nothing else seemed left to us but sickness, starvation and death itself. All we could do was to eat bark and roots and bitter berries that seemed to only make the hunger worse. Oh, sir, hunger is an

Angelique and Charlie wintered in a small log hut. Stonehouse Collection

awful thing. It eats you up so inside and you feel so all gone, as if you must go crazy. If you could only see the holes I made around the cabin digging for something to eat, you would think it must have been some wild beast. O'God, what I suffered there that winter from the terrible hunger, grace help me. I only wonder how I ever lived it through.

"Five days before Christmas (for you may be sure we kept account of every day) everything was gone. There was not so much as a single bean. The snow had come down thick and heavy. It was bitter, bitter cold and everything was frozen as hard as stone. We hadn't any snowshoes. We couldn't dig any roots; we drew our belts tighter and tighter; but it was no use; you can't cheat hunger; you can't fill up that inward craving that gnaws within you like a wolf.

"Charlie suffered from it even worse than I did. As he grew weaker and weaker he lost all heart and courage. Then fever set in; it grew higher and higher until at last he went clear out of his head. One day he sprang up and seized his butcher knife and began to sharpen it on a whetstone. He was tired of being hungry, he said, he would kill a sheep–something to eat he must have. And then, he glared at me as if he thought nobody could read his purpose but himself. I saw that I was the sheep he intended to kill and eat. All day and all night long I watched him and kept my eyes on him, not daring to sleep and expecting him to spring upon me at any moment; but after the fever fits were gone and he came to himself he was as kind as ever; and I never thought of telling him what a dreadful thing he had tried to do. I tried hard not to have him see me cry as I sat behind him, but sometimes I could not help it, as I thought of our hard lot and saw him sink away and dry up until there was nothing left of him but skin and bones. At last he died so easily that I couldn't tell just when the breath did leave his body.

"This was another big trouble. Now that Charlie was dead, what could I do with him? I washed him and laid him out but I had no coffin for him. How could I bury him when it was either rock or ground frozen as hard as a rock? And I could not bear to throw him out into the snow. For three days I remained with him in the hut and it seemed almost like company to me, but I was afraid that if I continued to keep up the fire he would spoil. The only thing I could do was to leave him in the hut where I could sometimes see him and go off and build a lodge for myself and take my fire with me. Having sprained an arm in nursing and lifting Charlie, this was very hard work but I did it at last.

"Oh, that fire, you don't know what company it was. It seemed alive just like a person with you, as if it could almost talk and many a time but for its bright and cheerful blaze that put some spirits in me, I think I would have just died. One time I made too big of a fire and almost burned myself out, but I had plenty of snow handy and so saved what I had built with so much labor and took better care for the future.

"Then came another big trouble–ugh, what a trouble it was–the worst trouble of all. You ask me if I wasn't afraid when left alone on that island. Not of the things you speak of. Sometimes it would be so light in the north and not even away up overhead like a second sunset, that the night seemed turned into day; but I was used to the dancing spirits and was not afraid of them. I was not afraid of the Mackee Monedo or Bad Spirit, for I had been brought up better at the mission than to believe all the stories that the Indians told about him. I believed that there was a Christ and that he would carry me through if I prayed to him. But the thing that most of all I was afraid of and that was that I had to pray the hardest against was this: Sometimes I was so hungry, so very hungry and the hunger raged so in my veins that I was tempted, oh, how terribly was I tempted to take Charlie and make soup out of him. I knew it was wrong, I felt it was wrong, I didn't want to do it, but some day the fever might come on me as it did on him and when I came to my senses I might find myself in the very act of eating him up. Thank God, whatever else I suffered I was spared that; but I tell you of all the other things that was the thing I was the most afraid and against which I prayed the most and fought the hardest.

"When the dreadful thought came over me, or I wished to die and die quick, rather than suffer any longer and I could do nothing else, then I would pray and it always seemed to me after praying hard something would turn up, or I would think of something that I had not thought of before and I have new strength given me to fight it out still longer. One time in particular I remember, not long after Charlie's death, when things were at their very worst. For more than a week I had nothing to eat but bark and how I prayed that night that the God would give me something to eat, lest the ever-increasing temptation would come over me at last. The next morning when I opened the door, I noticed for the first time some rabbit tracks. It almost took away my breath and made my blood run through my veins like fire. In a moment I had torn a lock of my hair out of my head and was plaiting strands to make a snare for them. As I set it, I prayed that I might catch a fat one and catch him quick. That very day I caught one and so raging hungry was I that I tore off his skin and ate him up raw. It was nearly a week before I caught another and so it was often for weeks together. The thing that seemed so very strange to me was though I had torn half the hair out of my head to make snares; never once during the whole winter did I catch two rabbits at one time.

"Oh, how heavily did the time hang upon me. It seemed as if the old moon would never wear out and the new one never come. At first I tried to sleep all that I could, but after a while I got into such a state of mind and body that I could scarcely get any sleep night or day. When I sat still for an hour or two, my limbs were so stiff and dried up that it was almost impossible for me to move them at all; so at last, like a bear in a cage, I found myself walking all the time. It was easier to walk than to do anything else. When I could do nothing else to relieve my hunger, I would take a pinch of salt. Early in March, I found a canoe that had been cast ashore, which I mended and made fit for use. Part of the sail I cut up and made the strips into a net. Soon the little birds began to come and then I knew that spring was coming in good earnest. God indeed had heard my prayer and I felt that I was saved. Once more I could see my mother.

"One morning in May, I had good luck fishing and caught no less than four mullets at one time. Just as I was cooking them for breakfast I heard a gun and fell back almost fainting. Then I heard another gun and I started to run down to the landing but my knees gave way and I sank to the ground. Another gun and I was off to the boat in time to meet the crew when they came ashore. The very first man that landed was Mendenhall and he put up his hand to shake hands with me, which I did. 'Where is Charlie' said he. I told him he was asleep. He might go to the hut and see for himself. Then they all ran off together. When Mendenhall went into the hut, he saw plain enough that I had not killed him, but that he had died of starvation. When I came up, Mendenhall began to cry and to try to explain things. He said that he had sent off a bateau with provisions and didn't see why they didn't get to us. But the boys told me it was all a lie. I was too glad to get back to my mother to do anything. I thought his own conscience ought to punish him more than I could do."[lviii]

Copper was king on the Keweenaw Peninsula and for a period, Isle Royale too! Shaft houses were a common sight. Stonehouse Collection

Several notes of explanation are in order. When the couple landed on the Isle Royale on July 1, they likely moved into an abandoned American Fur Company cabin on today's Mott Island. The "Mendenhall" in the story is Cyrus Mendenhall, one of the ten or so prospectors deeply involved in Keweenaw copper exploration at the time. The ten were later considered the great men in early mining.[lix] Among several ventures he was the agent and manager for a mine in Copper Harbor.[lx] Mendenhall was later involved in the famous Norwich Mine in Ontonagon County.[lxi] He also had a fairly extensive involvement with early treaty negotiation participating in the 1837/42 Mille Lacs Treaty and was a government signatory for the 1842 La Pointe Treaty.[lxii, lxiii]

Angelique was a full-blooded Native American, presumably Ojibwa. She was well equipped to deal with the harshness of nature as evidenced by her ability to construct a hut after the death of Charlie, fish, repair the canoe and construct rabbit snares.

Angelique was also likely not the author of the previous description of her experiences. The language is far too good for a mission school education. Probably she related the tale to

The mines followed the copper thousands of feet underground and required massive timber cribbing. Stonehouse Collection

someone else who in turn did the actual writing to include a fair amount of editing.

The real question is whether she did indeed "munch" on Charlie or not. There was considerable rumor afterward that she had, but noting the strong religious flavor of her story as befits a mission education, the deed was suppressed.

Considering that according to her story, by five days before Christmas they were completely out of food and reduced to eating tree bark and it wasn't until more than a week later she managed to snare a rabbit, clearly her food intake was at sub survival levels. It was also frequently several weeks between rabbits so unless the rabbits were the size of sheep; she was receiving another nutrient source. Remember too that leading up to running out of all food five days prior to Christmas she was on "short rations," and that she was burning a relatively high level of calories necessitated by cutting and hauling wood for the fire as well as just fighting the cold.

Had she succumbed to the overwhelming need to digest Charlie, it wasn't that unusual of an event. Cannibalism has a long tradition in the New World.

Some historians maintain the word itself was derived from the Carib Indians discovered by Christopher Columbus. The Carib were reputedly man-eaters and the Spanish name for them was Canibales, translating roughly as bloodthirsty and cruel. In some instances the consumption of the flesh was part of a religious ritual. The bodies of enemies were eaten to absorb their strength or those of ancestors so their spirits would live on in their new hosts. The Aztecs sacrificed thousands of people annually to their gods. Following the ceremonies the priest and others ate the bodies believing so doing brought them closer to the gods.[lxiv]

The butchered and cooked remains of seven people were recently discovered in a cooking pot in a 12th Century Pueblo village in Colorado. Key to the find was traces of human myoglobin, a protein found in human heart and skeletal muscle. Researchers concluded the village was the site of a cannibal feast.[lxv]

There are several references to cannibalism in the Jesuit Relations. These remarkable documents are the reports Jesuit

The Aztecs were reputedly man-eaters.
Stonehouse Collection

missionaries in New France sent to their superiors in the home country. Due to their rich and impressive descriptions and wealth of detailed observations, they were published and became widely read. The report from Father Ragueneau dated March 13, 1650 stated the Huron nation was plunged into distress and misery by war and famine. Two Jesuits, Charles Garnier and Noel Chabanel were killed at their mission. Ragueneau reported the famine was so severe cannibalism was practiced with corpses dug from their graves for food. As a result Jesuit fathers were forced to abandon their mission at Sault Ste. Marie and follow the Indians to St. Joseph Island at the south end of the St. Marys River.[lxvi]

A U.S. Topographic Engineer report in 1823 ascribed cannibalism to the Potawatomi, claiming they were driven to it by "hatred and resentment against all nations with they are at war." The report claimed the Indians acknowledged the action, as did various interpreters and traders.[lxvii]

When Pontiac's braves captured Fort Mackinac on King George's birthday, June 4, 1763, one witness claimed some of the attackers practiced cannibalism. As related in *Tuttle's Popular History of the Dominion of Canada*, nearly all the garrison was outside the fort walls watching a Lacrosse match between two Indian teams. When the ball rolled through the open fort gate, the Indians rushed in and using their tomahawks attacked the surprised garrison, murdering most of the English. Mr. Alexander Henry, an English trader, watched the butchery and resulting cannibalism. "Through an aperture which afforded me a view of the area of the fort, I beheld, in shapes the foulest and most terrible, the ferocious triumphs of barbarian conquerors. The dead were scalped and mangled. The dying were writhing and shrieking under the insatiable knife and tomahawk and from

The Jesuit Relations is a remarkable collection of historical material.
Stonehouse Collection

the bodies of some, ripped open, their butchers were drinking the blood scooped up in the hollow of joined hands, and quaffed amid shouts of rage and victory."[lxviii]

Another source relates that the Indians sometimes retained some of their prisoners for later mutilation and in the early days of Canadian exploration, occasional cannibalism. French soldiers were said to have witnessed the cooking and eating process.[lxix]

The French explorer Samuel de Champlain reported seeing an *Algonquin* war party return with numerous heads hanging from sticks on the front of their canoes as well as a dead body cut into quarters, which would be eaten in revenge.[lxx]

Jesuit missionaries were critical to the exploration of the New World. Stonehouse Collection

Cannibalism sometimes was the result of extremely dire circumstance. A story eerily similar to the Mott affair occurred in the Owen Sound area of Lake Huron roughly during the same period. As related by an early settler, "...an Indian, his squaw and two children, one of whom was a lad of thirteen or fourteen years of age, left Owen's Sound, on the Georgian Bay, Lake Huron, with the intention of traveling through the woods to Goderich, where a party of his friends were encamped for the winter.

"The snow was deep and the distance in a straight line, nearly eighty miles. It seems that, after crossing the river Saugeen, the weather became cloudy, attended by frequent snowstorms; so that they had nothing to guide them but the moss on the trees, for it appears they had never traversed that part of the country before. However, from some cause or another they lost their way; and their provisions also failed them. In this emergency they pitched their wigwam near a small stream, where they waited for several days, hoping the sun would make an appearance. To add to the difficulties of the miserable couple, their youngest papouse (sic), a girl, died from want and the hardships to which she had been exposed.

"Although the Indian had some ammunition, he was unable to find any game; not even a partridge. And the snow was so deep that it was quite impossible, in their exhausted state, to travel without snowshoes, especially.

"When they left Owen Sound there was not more than eight inches of snow, but in consequence of the continued fall it had increased to a depth of upwards of two feet. So when, at last, the weather cleared up they were totally unable to proceed.

"How long they remained in this dreadful situation is not easily known, but they were at last accidentally discovered by a party of French Canadians, who were out trapping, about twenty miles

Explorer Samuel de Champlain reported cannibalism. Stonehouse Collection

up from the Maitland, and who told me they were perfectly horrified at the scene that presented itself to their view. The old Indian and his squaw, wasted to perfect skeletons, were lying in the wigwam, unable to rise. Near these anatomies lay the remains of some human flesh that had evidently been used for food, and which the trappers positively declared to be part of the Indian's own son, who had been shot through the back by this wretched father, as he left the wigwam to go to the creek for water. Be this as it may, both the Indian and his squaw, when I questioned them on the subject after their recovery, denied it in the strongest terms.

"Whether the Indian killed his son to sustain this own life and that of his squaw, rests entirely on the assertion of the Canadians who found them, though I believe there is little doubt that in their extremity they made use of his flesh."[lxxi]

Early Hudson's Bay Company travelers claimed the Indians only resorted to cannibalism in the most dire circumstance. During one period of famine it was related that, "…they have become cannibals by necessity; and scarcely a month passes but some horrible tale of cannibalism is brought to the different establishments.[lxxii]

Charles F. Thuing in his book *Cannibalism in North America*, stated, "It is clear that the motives leading different races into the custom of devouring human flesh were different. With some it was eaten as food; with some it was eaten as part of a religious ceremony; with others it was eaten by reasons of superstition; and with yet others it was eaten as an act of vengeance to a fallen foe."[lxxiii] The Iroquois used ritual cannibalism, as did several other eastern tribes.[lxxiv] The Ojibwe, the predominant group in the Lake Superior region also practiced ritual cannibalism.[lxxv]

Eminent historian Frances Parkman, in *Pioneers of New France* stated, "Traces of cannibalism may be found among most of the North American tribes, though they are rarely very conspicuous. Sometimes the practice arose …from revenge or ferocity, sometimes it bore a religious character, as with the Miamis, among whom there existed a secret religious fraternity of man-eaters. Sometimes the heart of a brave enemy was devoured in the idea that it made the eater brave. "I will eat his heart," is by no means a mere figure of speech. The roving hunter-tribes, in their winter wanderings, were not infrequently impelled to cannibalism by famine.[lxxvi]

In circumstances of extreme duress the dead were a food source that allowed the survival of the living in many cultures. In November 1819 the Nantucket whaler *Essex* was sunk by a sperm whale in the Pacific. All 21 men in her crew abandoned her in three small 26-foot whaleboats. In an epic story of survival against all odds, two of the boats traveled nearly 4,500 miles over 89 days before finally being rescued. The third landed at a deserted island where they concluded death by starvation was their fate. The eight survivors of the *Essex* largely owed their lives to nourishment provided by the others. In some cases natural death provided a willing contributor. In others, straws were drawn to determine the victim and his killer. Surprisingly there was little social stigma when the men eventually returned to Nantucket. In fact, they were hailed as heroes. All returned to sea.[lxxvii] In another example when the Donner Party became stranded in the mountains of California during winter snows in 1846-47, half of the 87 people died. The remainder only survived by eating the dead.

Cannibalism continues in the world today. There are many stories coming out of the former Soviet Union and not just under threat of death by starvation. In 1996 ten people were charged in Perestroika with killing and eating other people. Police estimate 30 people were consumed. "We have information about cases where human flesh is sold in street markets. Every month we find corpses with missing body parts," stated a police official. Nikolai Dzhurmongaliev, Russia's most active cannibal is believed to have killed and eaten up to 100 women and served many to his neighbors in Kyargyzstan. Two women were said to provide enough meat for a week. To survive the long World War II siege of Leningrad by the Germans, it is claimed the defenders ate corpses. Of course we can't forget our own Jeffrey Dahmer who killed and ate 15 young men.[lxxviii] In 1972, 16 members of a Uruguayan soccer team survived for 70 days after their airplane crashed in the Andes Mountains by eating the remains of those that died in the crash. Under such conditions there is no shame in needed nibbling.

We shouldn't forget the Native American legend of the Windigo. When Angelique spoke of the "Bad Spirit" and being afraid of the "fever" coming on her, she was alluding in a fashion to the Windigo. The Windigo was the most dreaded spirit creature in the land. Cannibals, they struck from the north during the depth of winter, relentlessly hunting the weak and consuming them. Once possessed by a Windigo, ice grows inside the body and the face becomes hairy. The need for human flesh becomes overwhelming. It can infect people through a bite or a dream, transforming them into a zombie like state with a desperate craving for human flesh. When Angelique saw Charlie looking at her with the butcher knife did she not really see a Windigo? And was she not afraid of becoming one herself after his death?

After her ordeal at Isle Royale she soon regained her strength and tales are told that she once bet a French voyageur she could carry a heavy barrel of pork up a hill. The Frenchman was certain no mere squaw could accomplish such a feat! She easily won the bet and joked the next time he could ride on top of the barrel, deeply wounding Frog pride!

Angelique later worked as a cook for a Marquette, Michigan family and reportedly had periodic nightmares of her Isle Royale horror for the rest of her life. She died in Sault Ste. Marie in 1874. Regardless of whether Angelique consumed Charlie or not, her survival over the harsh Isle Royale winter, most of the time desperately hungry and alone, was an epic of endurance in the face of extreme adversity.

Fishermen's Wives

The wives of fishermen also knew the pain of death on the lakes.[lxxix] The number of small fishing boats lost on the Great Lakes is largely unknown, but the agony of the crew's families left behind was just as painful as the loss of a schooner or steamer.

On April 29, 1875 a fleet of fishing boats left St. Joseph for nearby fishing grounds. Although pieces of ice were still floating around on the lake, the crews had to make a living and that meant they needed to go fishing. The weather wasn't the best and old timers could sense a blow coming, but the consensus was they could do a lift before the bad weather hit. They were wrong. By the time they hauled their nets the wind had turned hard from the north and conditions were becoming very dangerous for the small boats.

One by one the fishing boats made St. Joseph harbor except for three; the *E.B. Perkins*, *Sea Gull* and *St. Joe Doll*, all perishing in the storm. Fred Dahlke and his three-man crew went down with the *Perkins*, Dahlke leaving a wife and five children. When the *Sea Gull* sank with captain Joseph Clamfoot, he left a wife and three children. Charles Witte, one of his two crewmen, left a wife and two children. When Captain Frank Groenke drowned with the *St. Joe Doll*, he left behind his wife Wilhelmina and two young children. His three-man crew were also lost.

The death of the fishermen impacted the small St. Joseph community greatly. A local committee started a subscription to provide some money for the families and even though supported generously by folks in Chicago too (which was a market for the St. Joe boats), it would not be enough to provide for the survivors. Fishing families had few resources. They always lived close to the edge. If fishing was good and prices high, they managed to put a little money aside. But the good times were rare. Usually it was a case of living and working on the edge, making do rather than climbing the economic ladder. Wilhelmina Groenke had a second chance however. Five months after her husband's death she married Robert Miller, a crewman on the fishing boat *Sarah*. It likely wasn't a love match, but rather one more of

Sail craft were common in the early days of commercial fishing. Stonehouse Collection

economic necessity. Wilhelmina and her children needed a provider and perhaps Miller needed a good woman. Regardless, within three weeks Wilhelmina was a widow again. The *Sarah* capsized entering the harbor in gale drowning Miller and the captain. There was no husband number three.[lxxx]

There Was An Old Woman Who Lived By the Lake

Rescue sometimes comes from the most unlikely places. The case of old Captain George McElroy of Port Huron is a case in point.

The captain was riding the *Scow No. 13* being towed by the tug *Bangs* west of Fairport, Ohio, Lake Erie on October 27, 1906 when a vicious 60 mile per hour gale parted the towline. The old captain had been in tight spots before so he just hung on and waited, figuring the scow would stay afloat long enough for the wind to blow him safely ashore. Or perhaps the Fairport Life-Saving Service crew would spot him and make the rescue.

However the wind shifted and blew the scow far offshore before it shifted around and pushed it closer to land. He was only about 2,000 feet off the Fairport breakwater before he finally spotted the lights of the city. The old navigator later reminisced, "That was when I began having the creeps and to think I was going to go if I washed in there. Its not a bad piece of wood at all, that old scow, but I knew that me and her'd be one if she ever got into that breakwater. And we seemed to be going in. I may have only been the way I felt and we might not have been drifting toward it at all, but I couldn't help thinking that we were. I could see the light in the lifesaving station and I pretty near fancied I could see the lookout man himself. I swung my light for an hour and a half as I've never swung a signal before. I thought sure they must see me but I guess they didn't." The fickle current pushed the scow safely past the threatening breakwater and into the black lake.

Every minute the captain expected he would see the life-savers jump into action and launch a boat but nothing happened. To see and not be seen in spite of your best efforts is supremely frustrating! Alone in the blackness, buffeted by the screaming wind and tossed by the wild seas, the captain hung on as the scow drove away from apparent safety.

Several hours later at about 7:00 a.m., the scow bumped on a sandbar, then hit again and again, each time rotating completely around. Finally, after rotating four times, it came hard on the beach, far enough up on the sandy shore to be relatively safe from the waves but still stranding the captain from dry land. A series of low hills separated beach from land.

About 10:00 a.m. a farmer's wife noticed his predicament. The captain later stated, "She was an old woman, but she was hefty and maybe she couldn't pull, but she stood on top of a hill and I thought she'd yank the shawl out through the air when I threw her a rope." With the woman holding fast, he was able to make his way to shore, ending his long ordeal.

The woman took him up to her farmhouse to warm up. "I always had a fancy for cider and ham and country eggs taste good any time. A little sail in the open on a raft is good for the appetite. Now that it's all over, I think I'd have enjoyed it if I'd been guaranteed that it would come out all right in the end." Worst of all however, in his excitement he couldn't remember the name of his rescuer! Her good deed is remembered but not her identity! [lxxxi]

Life-Saving Service

Women of course were never members of any U.S. Life-Saving Service crew. This was strictly a male occupation. That said however, women were "there," in the background, masked perhaps by the shadows, but they were "there."

Their most obvious contribution was via the Women's National Relief Association, organized in 1880. Often when victims were rescued, they were destitute, without even clothing. Organizations like the WNRA provided boxes of clothing station keepers could issue to victims when necessary. The organization collected clothing and shipped it to various stations to use as needed. Sometimes the victims remained at the station for weeks before transportation could be provided to get them home. At the station level, the keeper's wife usually took charge of the clothing box. The Life-Saving Service required the clothing to be carefully controlled by the keepers and noted in both the station log and official wreck reports but it was the women who did the work. If a shipwreck victim was fed from the station mess, regulations obligated the victim to pay for the meals. If the victim was destitute, the captain, owner or agent was billed 25 cents per head.[lxxxii] The station traveling library was also available for survivor use.

Organized in New York in 1880, the organization was very well politically connected. In 1882 Lucia Garfield, the wife of the President of the United States, was the president and the wife of the Chief Justice of the Supreme Court was the vice president. In 1909 the name was changed to the Blue Anchor Society, Aid to the Shipwrecked, Women's National Relief.

The wives of surfmen performed the critical job of supporting the men, especially during rescues. They built bonfires on the beach to guide the rescue boats back and provide illumination for beach work. They prepared coffee and food for rescuers and victims alike and prayed for their safe return. When the boats landed on the beach the women frequently rushed into the waves to help the occupants ashore. If men were injured, the wives nursed them back to health or grieved when death called. Should her surfman fail to return, she searched the lonely shore for his body.

Sometimes the captain's wife was even getting the job done before her husband knew exactly what was happening. For example, on September 12, 1902 the small schooner *Experiment* went up on the beach three-quarters of a mile north of St. Joseph harbor. The *Experiment* was on her way into the port during an especially black night when her captain was surprised by some off shore construction cribs and hastily turned to avoid a collision. Losing the wind, she drifted ashore. A sharp-eyed citizen saw the schooner's distress and notified the life-savers. Captain William Stevens soon pulled up next to the *Experiment* only to discover she was abandoned. Where was her crew? With nothing more to be done for her, Stevens returned to the station only to find six cold and wet sailors being thawed out by a roaring fire. His wife Ella was busy issuing clothing from the Blue Anchor box and preparing a warm meal. In turned out the crew had simply waded ashore and wandered along the beach until they found the station where Ella took charge. Captain Stevens didn't see them in the dark.

Fifteen years earlier Ella fed and clothed another shipwrecked crew, one that survived a more dangerous brush with disaster. About 1:30 a.m. on November 8, 1887 the schooner *Myosotis* was inbound just off the St. Joseph piers when a storm wave slammed her onto an outer sand bar. Several more waves shoved her off the shallows but unable to recover, she grounded about 150 yards from the beach. Captain Stevens and the life-savers responded quickly, launching his surfboat and pulling out to the wreck. However when rounding the rocky breakwater he saw the schooner's crew lowering their yawl.[lxxxiii] In spite of the dangerous seas, the yawl and its occupants safely made shore, the life-saving crew landing alongside them. Taking the survivors to the station, Ella fed them a hot meal and again broke out the "Blue Anchor" box![lxxxiv]

Two years later the South Haven Life-Saving Station had cause to break out their Blue Anchor box. About 2:00 p.m. on July 20 the wooden steamer *Joseph P. Farnam* was about 17 miles northwest of St. Joseph bound for Escanaba, Michigan. There was a considerable sea running down from the northeast and it was slow going, especially for an underpowered

Some of the woman living a lonely Vermilion Life-Saving Station. Stonehouse Collection

vessel like the *Farnam*. Captain Loren G. Vosburgh had just gone off watch and was fast asleep when his wife woke him asking, "What made it so smoky?" Quickly running on deck the captain discovered flames coming out of the engine room skylight! The mate was already dropping the fire hose but since the donkey engine to power it was engulfed in flames, it was a useless gesture. The captain turned next to the lifeboat but it was slung on falls abreast of the engine room, and in flames.

Knowing their only hope was to abandon ship quickly, he set the crew to work making rafts by lashing together hatch covers and planks. As soon as they were lowered over the side the crew and Mrs. Vosburgh followed. Four of the crew rode one raft and eight on the second. The eight-person raft remained tied to the ship until the hawser burned through. For a while it looked like the wind would drive the rafts toward South Haven but a shift to the southeast pushed them towards St. Joseph. They were close enough to shore to make out a large hotel and the pierhead light. The still burning steamer was driven to the northeast.

Their plight did not go unobserved. Shortly before 4:00 p.m. the surfman on watch in the South Haven lookout tower called Keeper McKenzie to look at a steamer on the western horizon than didn't look right. Both men watched the vessel carefully for half an hour with their glasses, finally concluding all was fine. A few minutes after the keeper left the tower the lookout noticed the steamer had lost her masts and immediately called the keeper back. Sensing there was an emergency, Keeper McKenzie ordered the crew called and ran to the harbor to engage a tug to tow the lifeboat out to the steamer. The strange vessel was a good dozen miles off shore and getting to her fast was critical, thus the tug was vital.

The only vessel available was the small steamer *Glenn* and her boilers were cold. On instructions from McKenzie the engineer went to work to fire up. At 6:00 p.m. there was enough pressure to get underway and with lifeboat in tow, she headed out for the steamer, now plainly identified as on fire. When the life-savers reached the steamer and discovered no one on board they immediately started a search. Somewhere there was a crew drifting around.

Wives worked hard to provide the best family life they could for their surfman, but it wasn't much that could be done. The cabin was at Point Betsie on Lake Michigan. Stonehouse Collection

Located on the desolate Lake Superior coast the life-saving service at Vermilion, Michigan was one of the most barren in the system. Some family shacks are on the extreme left. Stonehouse Collection

Just before dark McKenzie and his men sighted the two makeshift rafts and using the lifeboat, transferred everyone to the *Glenn*. The hastily made rafts were on the verge of disintegrating making it unlikely the *Farnam* crew would have survived until morning. Constantly doused by the waves and chilled by the wind, they were getting close to the end of their string. When they returned to the life-saving station Mrs. McKenzie broke open the Blue Anchor chest and distributed warm dry clothing and made sure everyone had a warm meal. The steamer crew lost everything in the fire. There was neither time nor room to take personal items. Doubtless Mrs. Vosburgh received her special care.[lxxxv]

The life-saving crews at South Haven, as well as most of the mainland stations were fortunate since they were able to keep their families nearby. The stations were either in town or just on the edge so while the government provided no family quarters, accommodation could be found locally. However at remote locations like Point Betsie or those along the infamous Lake Superior Shipwreck Coast, families had to find shelter in roughly built shacks made from shipwreck lumber. Certainly life in the remote stations was the most difficult. Some were located as far as

This group photo circa 1890, shows the life-saving families of Vermilion Point. Stonehouse Collection

40 miles from the nearest town and without the support of family or medical support, it was a hard situation for all.

Celia E. Persons, An Extraordinary Woman

The original *Women and the Lakes*[lxxxvi] book contained the story of Celia E. Persons, the wife of Thunder Bay Island Life-Saving Station keeper John Persons.[lxxxvii] Additional research has shed more light on the life of this remarkable woman.

Celia was born in Bath, Summit County, Ohio and attended Oberlin College near Cleveland. In 1872 she moved to Alpena, Michigan on Lake Huron, to teach music. There she met, fell in love with and married a young surfman from the Thunder Bay Island Life-Saving Station. On January 15, 1878 John was appointed keeper and Celia's life changed forever.

J.H. Persons was one of the legendary Great Lakes keepers. Stonehouse Collection

Celia Persons, a legend in her own right. Stonehouse Collection

John was born in Toledo, Ohio in 1851. He arrived at Thunder Bay with his father on a schooner seven years later. In 1861 his father became the Thunder Bay Island lightkeeper, providing John with a unique insight to the island, storms and shipwrecks. As a lightkeeper's son, it is likely he spent a great deal of time exploring the many reefs and shoals around the coast, gaining knowledge that would prove vital for his later life-saving career. When he was a teenager he witnessed the clear weather collision between the propellers *Pewabic* and *Meteor*, resulting in the loss of over 100 lives on the *Pewabic* when she plunged to the bottom. In 1877, at the youthful age of 26, John was appointed keeper of the Thunder Bay Island Life-Saving Station, replacing Isaac S. Mathews, fired by the Life-Saving Service for failing to vigorously go to the aid of the schooner *Charles Hinckley*. Keeper Mathews judged she was not in great danger but the Service concluded he should have investigated regardless. Failing to make a rescue was acceptable. Failing to try to make a rescue was not. It was a lesson John would remember. Prior to taking the keeper's sweep, John was captaining a fishing tug.

Thunder Bay Island Life-Saving station. Stonehouse Collection

Thunder Bay Island Station is located on Thunder Bay Island, about three miles east of Alpena, sitting right at the entrance to Thunder Bay. With John as a husband, Celia was given the opportunity to learn skills they didn't teach at Oberlin College. Running back and forth to the island in small boats taught her how to sail and navigate around the many dangerous reefs and shoals of the area and develop fine boat handling skills. Not bad for a music teacher!

Following shipwrecks, Celia had the unofficial duty of ministering to the needs of the victims. This was a leadership role the keeper's wife always assumed. She and the other life-saver's wives kept a bonfire roaring on the lonely shore and hot coffee and warm blankets ready for the survivors. Many a cold and miserable night was spent waiting for the surfboat to return through the stormy seas. Doubtless the women remembered times when the boats didn't come back.

John was involved in many shipwrecks and rescuing legions of sailors from difficult circumstances but likely one instance that was best remembered involved a Sunday school picnic in August 1892. The happy group was on the island when a seven-year-old boy fell off the dock and sunk to the bottom. John and a surfman ran to the dock, leaped into the water and hauled him to shore. A quick dose of the life-savers's famous "resuscitation of the apparently drowned" training restored him to life. With the youngster sputtering and coughing, Celia took over and gave him a set of dry clothes from her Blue Anchor chest.[lxxxviii]

Her talents also extended to being a midwife. On September 13, 1907 she officiated at the premature birth of a baby boy when the pregnant assistant lightkeeper's wife fell, triggering the event. The Thunder Bay Island Lighthouse was at the south end of the island and events moved too fast to bring a doctor from Alpena. John duly noted the event in the journal, claiming the station should receive credit for a life "saved."[lxxxix]

Celia also played the role of hostess to tourists that visited the island in the summer. It was later claimed that everyone along Huron's shore knew her. During the summer of 1911 a music professor from Detroit and several friends made a 1,300-mile motorboat tour of the lakes stopping at various places. At Thunder Bay Island they brought their trusty phonograph ashore and gave "concerts" with it. While the professor reported the life-savers enjoyed the new "ragtime" pieces, they were most enthralled by the classics, particularly music from "Lucia" and the "William Tell Overture." Before the professor and his boat left, Celia furnished them with fresh bread, pies, a can of milk and other delicacies.[xc] Obviously the old music teacher reacted favorably to the new "technology."

She and John had two children; a son Byron H. and a daughter Nina. Celia home schooled both and they later attributed much of their success in life to her teaching skills as well as growing up on the island.

Perhaps her most remarkable achievement was gaining her captain's license. John was a master boat builder and saw a need for a small steamer to ease travel. When he finished the steam yacht *Florence C.* in 1889, he promptly took out the required papers to be her engineer. Celia however, took and passed the difficult master's exam. When the *Florence C.* steamed over Thunder Bay, John tended the boiler but Celia was "wheel'n."

Celia and John had a unique experience harking back to the *Pewabic* so many years before. Because the propeller carried a rich cargo of copper ingots when she sank, the vessel was a target for salvage. In 1895 John assisted the American Wrecking and Salvage Company to locate her and as a recognition, he, Celia, their daughter Nina and several others were in turn, lowered to the wreck in a diving bell. Celia's comments were not recorded but John later recalled, "I saw her lying on the bottom of the lake, 160 feet down. The old *Pewabic* was a green ship lying in a bed of white sand… We went from bow to stern and all around her in the diving bell."[xci]

Celia died from pneumonia on January 12, 1912 in Port Huron, Michigan. She was 59 years of age. Celia and her husband were in Detroit for the wedding of their daughter on December 30. From there they traveled to Harbor Beach, Michigan to attend the reception for Captain Jerome Kiah on January 3. While returning from this event she suddenly became ill and when the train reached Port Huron she was taken to the home of Homer Plough, an old family friend and the son of Life-Saving Service captain George Plough, where she succumbed. George Plough was also John's cousin.

The gathering she and John attended at the Dow House at Harbor Beach was a very special event. Twenty life-saving station keepers, many with their wives, came together to honor the district superintendent, Jerome Kiah. A legendary life-saver, he also was the sole survivor of a terrible disaster in April 1879. While heading for a schooner in distress off Point aux Barques, the station surfboat capsized in the waves. Although the crew righted it, she rolled again and again. Eventually all of the men succumbed to the frigid water except for keeper Kiah. Somehow he alone survived. Although the invitations were issued earlier in the year, the event was kept secret from him to preserve the surprise. All the keepers were in full uniform and the banquet

Jerome Kiah was the sole survivor of a disastrous April 1879 rescue attempt. All of his crew save he, were lost. Stonehouse Collection

considered very elegant. Keepers traveled from afar to attend, including distant stations at Duluth, Portage and Marquette.

John Persons acted as toastmaster for the event. Considered the "dean" of the keepers based on his 34 years of service, it was a rich honor for he and Celia. All of the men and wives were their friends and contemporaries, perhaps none better than Jerome Kiah.

In Celia's obituary the local paper reported that, she was, "…one of the greatest life savers on the Great Lakes and to the women of the service deep tribute is due. To hundreds of shipwrecked sailors she had administered. She fed, clothed and gave them succor. The blackest fireman, the ordinary deckhand and the master of a big steamer all looked alike to her–human beings in distress. And to the thousands of visitors at Thunder Bay she was ever the gentile hostess to make you welcome. All along the Great Lakes hundreds of miles either way, there are men and women who almost feel as if a calamity had befallen the service."

"Simple services were held from the home of Mr. and Mrs. Byron N. Persons Sunday afternoon. The Congregational choir sang. There were many old friends of the family present to pay their last respects to a woman whom honor was due. There were many beautiful floral tributes, not only from Alpena but also from Detroit, Port Huron, Harbor Beach and other places."[xcii]

Life-Saving captains from as far as Two Heart River and Vermilion Point on Lake Superior made the long, sad trip to

Alpena. As they had banded together such a short time before to honor Jerome Kiah, they assembled again to support John Persons in his bereavement. Life-saving keepers were a rare breed. Tested by storm and gale as they led their crews to dramatic rescues, they were a true fraternity of "Heroes of the Surf." They were men who had looked death in the eye, again and again. Such a bond was incredibly strong.

After the funeral John returned to his home on Thunder Bay Island for the rest of the winter. It was the home where Celia and he had lived all their married life, spending the long winters isolated from the world. They had their books, children and each other. What more could they want? Doubtless it was now very empty and he must have missed Celia terribly. Following her death a small item appeared in the newspaper mentioning a surfman Brown and his wife would be spending the winter on Thunder Bay Island and they would be the only people there other than John. Although unstated in any record I could locate, I do believe the Browns just didn't want the old keeper to be alone during such a difficult period. Such loyalty is both remarkable but for John and Celia, common too![xciii]

John suffered another blow in April 1913. Homer Plough, in whose home Celia died, passed on himself. He was only 34 years old and left a wife and two children. John was unable to attend the funeral as he was trapped on Thunder Bay Island by spring ice.

Isle Royale Women

Women on Isle Royale were relatively rare, but there were some in the early mining days and during the commercial fishing period. If properly provisioned, people were able to survive the winter, although fighting boredom was always a challenge.

Lydia Douglass, whose husband worked for the Ohio and Isle Royale Company, spent the period 1848-49, on the island, living near today's Rock Harbor. Certainly Angelique Mott's ordeal was fresh in her mind. During the spring and summer there were many distractions available to compensate for the remote location. She went sailing in a small boat and often gathered berries from the many small islands as well as carried picnic lunches to remote locations. Often she visited with other women including Cornelius Shaw's wife and Mrs. Mark Mathews, the wife of a company manager, when she came to the island with her husband. If the men were not available to take the women out on an exploring trip, a Metis (mixed blood Indian woman), acted as their guide. Frequently they returned with agates and wild flowers, treasures from the wilderness. The women felt proud to manage such trips without their men folk.

When winter set in, opportunities for travel and visiting vanished and everyone just "hunkered down" to survive the dark and cold. Lydia Douglass occupied her days with reading and sewing, activities well suited to whittle away the long winter days snowbound in their cabin. Luckily her husband had carried a small but full library with him thus providing a long winter's distraction.[xciv]

Much of the population at this time centered on Ransom, near the present day Daisy Farm. Roughly fifty people called it home and the settlement included a log office and storehouse, blacksmith shop, furnace, smelter and dwelling house. The cabin Lydia stayed in was described as large, having eight rooms on the first floor. A dock on Rock Harbor provided the lifeline to the outside world, but only when the boats ran.

During the 1870s, conditions on the island were not much different. The work force was largely made up of Irish, Germans, French-Canadians, Swedes, Norwegians, Finns and native-born Americans. It was a reflection of the general mixed Keweenaw population. As in the Keweenaw copper and the Michigan Iron Range, the key men were the Cornishmen. Specially recruited from Cornwall, England, they were the real miners, men who knew the secrets of hard rock mining. The Cornish were the captains and crew leaders. They alone had the skills required to sink the shafts and cut the drifts needed to make the rock "pay." Everyone else was secondary to the skills the Cousin Jacks brought to the job.

Sarah Barr Christian, the wife of a mine official, wintered on the island in 1874-75. She noted the Swedes and Norwegians did most of the surface jobs other than the woods work the Finns excelled at. A constant supply of wood was needed for both underground and surface construction as well as firewood. Local Indians supplied the fish and game and made sugar maple in the spring. Although "rough and ready," she didn't consider it a bad life.

Being in the midst of such a remote, male dominated frontier society was a new experience for Sarah but one she likely thrived on. Everything was new, from the babble of strange language to the interaction with the Indians. Like Lydia of a generation before, surviving the winter meant hunkering down with a good book. Options for other activities were limited, but certainly short snowshoeing adventures were possible as was ice fishing.

By the last period of mining activity life on the island improved significantly. With the advent of modern steel freighters supplies were delivered with greater regularity, deeper into the winter and earlier in the spring. During the depth of winter, residents at Washington Harbor at the south end of the island ventured out to ice skate, snowshoe and toboggan. The resident doctor also officiated at the birth of at least one child during the winter of 1891. Indians using dogsleds delivered mail.

Commercial fishing was an island activity dating from the days of the old American Fur Company. When the fur began to run out, the company shifted to commercial fishing. Under the best of circumstances commercial fishing is a difficult and dangerous way to earn a living. While the fishing grounds at Isle Royale were rich and productive, the remoteness of the island, difficulty in marketing the catch and dangerous weather all made the operation arduous at best.

Fishing was also a family enterprise. To be successful, all members, husband, wife, children and other relatives had to work together. Even then there was no guarantee of success. While the men went out and set nets and hauled fish, the women managed the household, mended the nets and assisted with packing the catch. During winter, ice blocks were cut out of the lake, hauled to a communal icehouse and packed away in sawdust insulation until summer. Prior to electric refrigeration ice was critical to store and ship the catch. The family worked from before dawn to after sunset. What ever needed to be done was done. It was that simple.

Although the number changed over time, in 1929 there were 75 fishing families on the island, about 250 people. Most of the catch was shipped to Chicago by lake steamers like the *America*. Times were good with lots of fish and a ready market. When the stock market crashed in October everything changed.

Some families wintered over on the island to save money during the Depression. The families usually maintained two residences. A "real" home on the mainland and a fish camp on the island. Selling or renting the mainland home was a method of raising cash. During the winter of 1932-33, schoolteacher Dorothy P. Simonson was employed at Chippewa Harbor as schoolteacher for the children of fisherman Holger Johnson. Holger had five children and convinced the Keweenaw County School Commissioner that his children deserved a teacher just like the kids on the mainland. Johnson supplied the schoolhouse and the County provided $25 for supplies. Dorothy lived in a small log cabin together with her six-year-old son. The only students were Johnson's five and Dorothy's son for a total of six. While she spent her days in the classroom, her nights were used for reading and writing her diary. To keep back the cold, she also devoted a considerable amount of time hauling "hundred-pound chunks of wood for that round, black, devil of a stove." When school ended in the spring she was anxious to get off the island as fast as possible but also introspective enough to wonder at how fast the school year passed. In spite of Johnson's requests for additional teachers, the County usually refused to support them, not desiring to encourage development of a year around fishing community that would be expensive to maintain. However occasionally teachers were provided but only rarely.[xcv]

Wireless Women

History can be tantalizing in what it reveals or perhaps more often, what it just shows a little piece of. For example, a November 1906 item in the *Detroit Free Press* mentioned, "Chicago, October 31, - Wireless telegraphy will this winter form one of the courses taught at the nautical school conducted by Lieut. W. J. Wilson in the Masonic Temple. At the first session last night telegrams were sent from one room to another by means of a small machine and the would be captains were set to work figuring out the intricacies of the Morse telegraph code. The school now has forty-six students enrolled. One woman has joined the class and several more will enter later." What happened to them? One would think that considering the temper of the times, being a "wireless" operator would be a natural occupation for a woman.

Full Circle

Females have always been prescribed from a combat role in the U.S. Navy. It was only in comparatively recent times they were allowed to serve at all. Nevertheless, when the nation called, the women answered.

Before the U.S. Navy existed, women worked to achieve the country's independence. An estimated 20,000 helped the Continental Army as spies, cooks, nurses or just plain camp followers. A few, if the stories are to be believed, disguised themselves as men and served in the ranks. Since the beginning the Navy had rules prohibiting women aboard ships. A new set of regulations in 1802 allowed the captain to transport women if he had orders to do so from his squadron commander. That year Commodore Richard V. Morris in the frigate *Cheaspeake* took along his wife, infant son and black maid when he led his squadron to the Mediterranean. He allowed some of the crew's wives along too. When the inevitable happened and a woman went into labor, the ship's doctor ordered her placed near the guns and a broadside fired to speed delivery. This was a common practice aboard ship and was one of the explanations for the old expression, "son of a gun." In 1813 Commodore Stephen Decatur brought two women aboard the frigate *United States* as nurses in anticipation of combat casualties. Both were wives of crewmen and had no medical training.[xcvi]

The tale of Lucy Simpson is most endearing whether true or false. According to legend, as a 16-year-old Lucy was seduced by a sailor and left pregnant. The child died at birth. Shunned by her family, she took up work in a Boston brothel where in 1812 she met a Navy lieutenant who told her about Deborah Sampson, an English girl who disguised herself as a man and served both the British Navy and Army from 1745-50. The lieutenant implied she could do the same, signing on to the *Constitution* then in port. According to the legend, Lucy dressed in a sailor's suit and joined up as a marine. Since ships carried many young boys, her fair features didn't arouse suspicion and she fought in three battles after which she returned to her home and wrote her memoirs, which became a bestseller. Let unsaid was her relationship with the lieutenant aboard the ship. After all, he knew her secret and he did meet her in a brothel![xcvii]

The Navy continued to experience challenges with women afloat, especially when captains brought their wives along on extended deployments. In 1838 Commodore Isaac Hull took his wife and her sister with him to the Mediterranean. The wife caused no trouble but the sister was a "handful." The officers rebelled against her disruptive influence and it was claimed riots, desertion and insubordination were the result. Regardless of size, a ship is a very small place and it is easy to imagine how one troublemaking woman can cause the pot to boil over. In 1842 Congress directed the Secretary of the Navy to publish regulations prohibiting captains from taking their wives aboard ships. But it wasn't until 1881 all women were finally excluded.[xcviii]

During the Civil War the Army used several vessels as floating hospitals and employed female nurses aboard. While the Navy still resisted women afloat, in 1869 some were working as cooks and cleaning women at the Navy Asylum in Philadelphia. Ten years later a woman was employed as a writer in the Hydrographic Office to soon be followed by women draftsmen, telegraph operators, clerks, copyists, etc.[xcix] It was progress of a sort.

During the rapid growth of the Navy for World War I, women were accepted for the first time in the Reserves and allowed to perform the same jobs as men, at least as yeomen, the Navy's equivalent of clerks. Officially designed "Yeomen (F)," it was

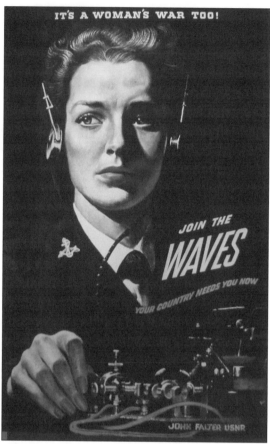

IT'S A WOMAN'S WAR TOO!

JOIN THE

WAVES

YOUR COUNTRY NEEDS YOU NOW

JOHN FALTER USNR

The Navy made an effort to recruit women of the Navy. Stonehouse Collection

soon corrupted into "yeomenette." The "F" of course meant female. Although the job wasn't very glamorous, it did free men for assignment to combat duty. The women also worked as secretaries, telephone operators, radio operators, finger printers and a few in the intelligence field. After the war the program was ended and women were no longer allowed in "this man's Navy."

With the outbreak of World War II, the Navy again needed women and they again answered the call and joined the Navy Reserve. This time they were called WAVES (Women Accepted for Voluntary Emergency Service). The first WAVES arrived at the Great Lakes in November 1942. The first WAVE to report was an Ensign Knight assigned to work in the Ninth Naval District Security Office. By the end of the month another dozen officers and 23 enlisted WAVES arrived. By January the following year, nearly 700 enlisted women were assigned to the base, freeing up the men for fleet assignment. The WAVES proved to be a great asset, managing the mail, running communications centers, teaching chemical warfare, aviation gunnery, instrument flying and parachute rigging. After the war, the WAVES program was disbanded and the women released. Times were changing however and the women did not go meekly back into society. Many wanted to continue their Navy careers and pressured Congress to pass the Women Services Integration Act of 1948. On June 12 of that year the first recruit school for women was established at Great Lakes. Today women are students in every part of the center as well as serving in command and staff positions.[c]

As a mark of how change has indeed occurred, on August 21, 2004 Captain Kathryn M. Hobbs assumed command of Naval Station Great Lakes. An officer with wide experience, she had previously served on the staff of the Naval Education and Training Command, taught Naval ROTC at the University of San Diego, Executive Officer Naval Support Activity, Diego Garcia, British Indian Ocean Territory and Chief of Staff for the Commander, Fleet Air Mediterranean in Naples, Italy among other assignments.[ci]

From simple clerks in World War I, to base commander in 2004, women at Naval Base, Great Lakes have come a very long way!

CHAPTER FIVE

LIGHTHOUSE KEEPERS

A Wandering Life–Anna Maria Carlson

Anna Maria Carlson was the wife of Robert Carlson, who started his career at Outer Island in the Apostle Islands as the second assistant keeper in November 1891. He later became the principal keeper at nearby Michigan Island in August 1893, moving to Marquette in May 1898 and finally Whitefish Point from 1903 until his retirement in 1931. All the lights were on Lake Superior.

Michigan Island Light, Anna's first posting as a lightkeeper's wife, was a lonely place, especially for a girl from the city. The light at Michigan Island was also a confusing situation. When the contractor's crew arrived to build it in 1856 they were somehow convinced to erect it on Michigan Island instead of the Lighthouse Board's intended location of Long Island. There is some speculation that it was the local inspector who countermanded the original instructions or perhaps the company just felt it was a better location and changed it on their own authority. Regardless the small one and a half story stone lighthouse with attached tower was built in the "wrong" place. It only operated for a year before being decommissioned and the government apparently forced the contractor to build a new lighthouse on Long Island in compensation for the original "error." In 1869 the Lighthouse Service decided the original light was needed and arranged for it to be refurbished and equipped with a three and a half order Fresnel

Michigan Island was a lonely and desolate place. Stonehouse Collection

lens. This was the light where Anna and Robert were stationed. By 1919 the Lighthouse Board decided a new light was needed and when the Schooner's Ledge Light at the Delaware River in Pennsylvania was discontinued the old steel tower was disassembled and shipped to Michigan Island. However the pieces lay on the beach open to the effects of weather until 1929 when it finally was erected.

Anna was born in Sweden and immigrated to the United States as a teenager. She married Carlson, just appointed second assistant at Outer Island, at age 21. She had many adventures during her marriage and after Robert retired in 1931 related some to a reporter from the *Detroit News.*

"I had three persons to talk to: my husband, who was assistant keeper, the head keeper, an old man (authors note, the keeper was John Leonard, principal keeper 1888-1896) with but one eye and a fisherman who came that summer and lived in a shack down the shore. (Authors note, it is curious Anna didn't mention Emmanuel Luick, who was first assistant and was also at the lighthouse at this time.)

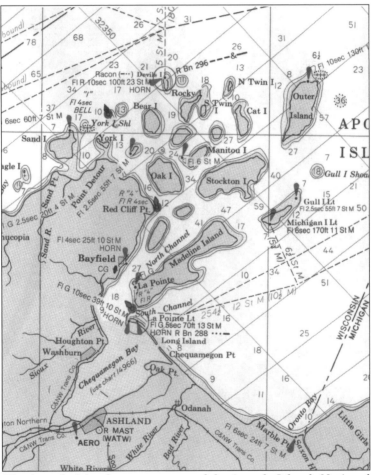

The Apostle Islands are now part of the Apostle Islands National Lakeshore but a century ago they were a desolate part of the Lake Superior Coast. Stonehouse Collection

Anna Carlson led a "wandering" life as the wife of lightkeeper Robert Carlson.
Stonehouse Collection

"Oh! The loneliness of those days on Outer Island! There was nothing to see but water, with the dim outline of other islands of the Apostles group behind the haze and an occasional steamer way out on the lake. When my housework was done, my husband used to take me down the shore to the fisherman's shack, where we would visit for a while. Or we would walk out into the woods.

"That was my life, day in and day out. Going ashore to the mainland, 40 miles away, meant riding in a sailboat, which always frightened me. Nights I would look out of the window and see nothing but the dark water; no lights anywhere, not even in the fisherman's shanty, which was too far away.

"The old lighthouse keeper (Leonard), dead these many years, was always very kind. He showed me how to cook, for I had never been used to much work. I have learned to do all kinds of housework since my marriage. A woman can learn to do anything if she sets her mind to it.

Loneliness was one thing but pure fear was another. Sometimes events can take a very sudden and deadly turn especially at an isolated Lake Superior lighthouse.

"We were trying a winter on Michigan Island where my husband was head lighthouse keeper. His brother was assistant (authors note, the employment records do not support this). When we decided to stay, our hired girl promised to remain with us through the winter. But she slipped away and went ashore with some fishermen and didn't come back.

"(One day) they (her husband and his brother) took the dogs and went fishing. I was always afraid to be left alone on the island. A city-bred girl, the stark loneliness of it was appalling. As soon as they left the house I ran about and locked all the doors and windows. Yet there was nobody on the island but myself and the children, a little girl past two and the twin boys, nine months old.

"For a few hours after they had gone that day I was busy settling the house in order. The tower was closed but there was lots of work to do in the house and I was glad for that. I got the children's lunch, prepared things for an early supper, as I knew the men would be hungry when they came home and then sat down to wait.

"Women who wait in brightly lighted cities with people all around within call of the voice have no conception what it is like to sit and wait for your man on a deserted island, with snow and ice everywhere and no light but the stars.

"I watched the sun go down across the water, waited until it's sickly yellowish light had disappeared and the stars came out. I kept stoking the fires, for I knew the men would be cold when they came in.

"I did not even think of such a thing as their not coming. They had been gone since before daylight and they would be home before six, I was sure. The wind was blowing a gale, but in my ignorance of such things I gave it no thought.

"Six o'clock came and darkness. It was so dark outside I could not bear to look out the window, but kept watching for the men and the dogs. It began to snow. Seven o'clock and still my man had not come. I put the children to bed and waited."

What Anna didn't know was the ice had broken up and the men were trapped on an ice sheet heading out into the lake!

"All night long I sat by the fire, terror clutching my heart. I could not believe they would not come. Every time the wind rattled the branches of the trees around the lighthouse I would start up, expecting to hear my husband's voice."

The next morning Anna was faced with the problem of feeding the younger children which meant milking the cow in the barn. Surprisingly this was a job Robert always did and while she watched a couple of times, it was a task she had never done. Unable to approach the cow directly, she chopped a hole in wall next to the stall and reaching through the hole, managed to coax enough milk from the cow to feed her children. Back at the house she continued to wait and watch throughout the day and long night. No one came.

"Things began to get a little hazy after that. Two nights of terror and another night faced me. Somehow I lived through them, looked after the children, got their milk, fed the chickens. That is about all I remember of those days.

"It seemed hours afterward that I came back to the house. The twins were asleep in the cradle. Little sister was rocking them. As I closed the door, I fell to the floor screaming. I screamed at the top of my voice, until I was exhausted. And still my husband did not come. There was another terrible night before me.

"You know how it is with us women. Sometimes when we think we can't endure any longer, it does us good to let go, like that. I think if I had not screamed I would have lost my mind.

"That night I slept a little. On the fourth day the weather had cleared but it was still bitterly cold. I went about the house in a daze. The same chores had to be done, the children had to be cared for. How I hated Lake Superior!"

While Anna fought her own demons, Robert and his brother were fighting for their lives. When the storm came up unexpectedly it broke the ice sheet they were on from the main piece, sending them drifting out into the open lake. The men, sled and dogs all waited for their fate. Eventually the sheet smashed into Madeline Island and the men and dogs were able to struggle to shore. There they discovered some flour in a fisherman's shanty along with dry wood and kindling. Once a fire was roaring along nicely they cooked up

Robert Carlson had a difficult tenure in Marquette. Stonehouse Collection

a thin gruel from ice and flour. Then they hunkered down to wait out the storm. When the weather cleared they managed to patch an old boat they found on the beach and used it to row the eight miles back to Michigan Island.

The men had suffered badly from the cold, as did the dogs. It took two weeks for Robert and his brother to recover, which meant more work for Anna. One of the trusty dogs was so injured he had to be put down. Never again did the Carlsons try to winter over at a lighthouse![cii]

Robert and Anna had a particularly ugly experience while stationed at Marquette Light. The lighthouse and U.S. Life-Saving Station shared the general area on Lighthouse Point. In fact the preponderance of the land was lighthouse reservation with a much smaller part, perhaps an acre or so of the nearly eight-acre total,

Marquette lighthouse as it appeared when Carlson was keeper.
Stonehouse Collection

being used by the life-savers. Having a lighthouse and life-saving station so close sometimes caused conflict. There was tendency for the lightkeepers to see themselves as the landlord and the life-savers as unruly tenants.

When Robert Carlson transferred to Marquette Harbor Light from Michigan Island Light in 1898 he moved from an environment in which he was "king" of his own island. He was the lord of the manor. It was also a very lonely place with few actual people underfoot. By contrast, Marquette was a city of thousands, many of which enjoyed visiting the lighthouse grounds. This was definitely not to Carlson's liking and even worse from his perspective, the Lighthouse Service encouraged such visits in the name of good public relations!

There is no record of Anna's thoughts about the change but judging from her comments about life in the lonely Apostles, Marquette must have been a joy! A library, theater, lectures, dances, schools, streetcars, all at her doorstep! Her husband apparently viewed it all very differently.

Lighthouse Point could be a dangerous play area for a keeper's children. The rocky point juts out into the lake and footing was often difficult. Just a day after they arrived, one of the Carlson children slipped on the rocks and broke her arm.

Carlson seems to have been a complex character. From old log book entries it is clear he was friendly with Henry Cleary the Life-Saving Station keeper, the two spending time repairing various boats, fishing and even owning a small launch together. When the water intake for the City Water Works, which is adjacent to the lighthouse grounds, froze during the especially cold winter of 1900, he worked for ten days helping to thaw it out. Friendly with the plant superintendent, he was willing to lend a hand in getting the problem fixed. When it froze up again a couple of days later, he spent another five days thawing it out. However he seems to have had trouble with those he considered subordinate to him. For example, assistants didn't stay long, either resigning or transferring elsewhere.[ciii]

During the summers Lighthouse Point became a popular area for picnics and as a matter of policy, the Lighthouse Service encouraged such activity as good public relations. On some weekends hundreds of people crowded the lighthouse grounds, which created additional work for Carlson to prevent damage and answering questions. Some of the visitors built small fires to either cook with or as nighttime campfires. Carlson expressed concern that one could burn out of control and threaten the lighthouse so in June 1903 he wrote to the District Inspector requesting authority to ban both fires and picnicking. The Inspector approved Carlson's request. Judging from period photographs of the lighthouse grounds it is difficult to understand Carlson's concern about fires as the point was virtually denuded of vegetation. Virtually all lighthouse grounds were "clear cut" to allow maximum visibility without the hindrance of shrubs, trees or tall grass. Clearly his real motive was to keep visitors away from "his" lighthouse.[civ]

On July 6, 1903 Carlson discovered a group of picnickers including David Shelton, the number two surfman at the life-saving station, gathered around a bonfire. The keeper told the group such

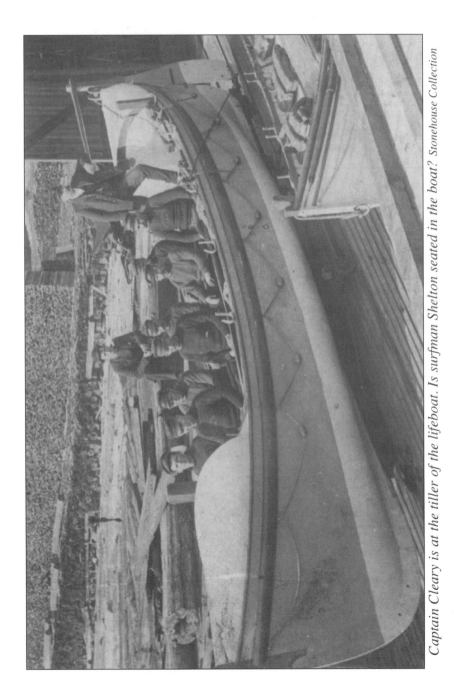

Captain Cleary is at the tiller of the lifeboat. Is surfman Shelton seated in the boat? Stonehouse Collection

fires were prohibited, kicked the fire out and sent them packing. The following morning Carlson and his assistant were walking to the breakwater when Shelton approached and assaulted the keeper, or so Carlson recorded in his log. The licking the surfman gave Carlson was thorough. He was struck about the head so severely he was forced to take to his bed and there was some doubt he would regain the sight of one eye. As his assistant simply stood by as Shelton beat Carlson, the keeper believed he was "in on" the attack, so he designated Anna to take over his duties rather than the assistant. She also had to care for her bed-ridden husband and family.[cv]

Shelton apparently was never punished in any way for the assault which leads to the question of whether Carlson "deserved" the beating. Did he provoke Shelton? Were Carlson's actions in dousing the fire and throwing the picnickers off the point the previous day so offensive, Shelton felt he had to respond? Considering that Cleary and Carlson were supposed to be friends, would not Cleary have punished Shelton for such an attack? Why would Carlson not pursue criminal action against his assailant? There are questions, but no answers.

After the incident it was necessary to "get Carlson out of town." His efforts to drive tourists from Lighthouse Point had clearly made enemies. A new more socially skilled keeper was needed. A switch was engineered with Charles Kimball, the keeper at Whitefish Point at the east end of Lake Superior. By October both men were in their new jobs. Kimball and his family enjoyed the more urban environment of Marquette while the Carlsons' returned to the remote life. There is no record of Anna's thoughts of having the luxuries of Marquette so suddenly yanked away and banishment to the wilds of Whitefish Point.

Regardless of his proclivities, Carlson was a brave man and at Whitefish Point he lead a valiant rescue. In 1914 he and two fishermen used the keepers boat to rescue eleven men from a capsized launch. There is some question whether the fishermen actually volunteered to or not. One version of the incident claims Carlson obtained their services only when he threatened them with his revolver![cvi]

Robert Carlson and his wife Anna on their retirement at Whitefish Point.
Stonehouse Collection

Robert and Anna retired from the Lighthouse Service from Whitefish Point on April 1, 1931. They purchased a home in Sault Ste. Marie and settled down for a well-deserved rest.

"I Hate Lighthouses"

Another lighthouse keeper's wife also disliked the job intensely. Cecelia Carlson McLean was Robert Carlson's sister. In 1898 she married keeper Alexander McLean. Interviewed in 1931 she was very candid in describing her extreme dislike of the duty.

"I hate lighthouses. They are so lonely, going from one island to another, out in the Apostles group, isn't much fun, especially when you have to go in a small boat and maybe get caught in a storm. We left Raspberry Island in 1916 and I was glad enough to see the last of it.

"When a woman marries a lighthouse keeper, she gives up everything else in the world. If I had my life to live over again, it would not be in lighthouse stations.

"My husband was 35 years in the lighthouse service. Thirty of those I was his wife, living on the isolated stations in the Apostle Islands and part of the time at Two Harbors, Minnesota, where one might as well be on an island for all the social life one is able to have. Winters I was shut in by unbroken snowdrifts down in the railroad yards which shut off the lighthouse from the town and while the men folks got the children out to school and back, by the time I was ready to go anywhere the roads were drifted full again. And ma could stay home. There was always too much to do around home anyway, to spend any time getting to town.

"On the islands we always had to keep up two homes, as women and children have to be off the islands October 15 and when you have two homes to maintain, something has to be slighted. We slighted necessities. Luxuries–we had none of them. We gave up the things we needed."

Cecelia honeymooned on Devils Island, surely a strange place to take a new bride. "In storms the spray used to dash against my living room windows, 600 feet from the cliffs and ooze through the

Devils Island lived up to it's forbidding name. Stonehouse Collection

windows and flood the floor so that I would have to take rags and sop it up. Such a mess it always made." She also remembered, "I spent six years on that island. Tourists used to come from Bayfield and that was all the social contact I had. We always seemed to be at lonely outposts. There were three years on Huron Island, three miles offshore from the Keweenaw Peninsula (author's note–she misspoke. It is off the Michigan mainland) and when my husband was on Stannard Rock I had to live alone on the mainland. (Author's note–Alexander does not appear on the list of keepers for the Rock) We're through with lighthouses now and I am glad."

Alexander had been a lighthouse keeper for five years when he finally married. He started his career in November 1895 as an assistant keeper at Isle Royale Light on lonely Menagerie Island. He served as keeper of the Eagle Harbor Range Lights for three weeks in May 1898 before moving to Michigan Island Light in the Apostles for five months, leaving in October 1898 for the job at Devils Island and a brand new wife. In June 1909 they moved to nearby Raspberry Island, then to Huron Island in 1916 remaining

Nearby Raspberry Island was likely a better assignment than Devils Island. Stonehouse Collection

Two Harbors must have seen to be heaven sent compared to some of the isolated stations. National Archives

until 1919 when the couple transferred to Two Harbors, Minnesota. Alexander retired in 1931.[cvii]

By contrast Alexander liked the life, saying if he didn't he "…would not have spent 35 years keeping the lights going."[cviii]

A Filthy Mess

The difficulty for a keeper and his family to just get to some lights is clearly explained in this reminiscence from Edna Lane Sauer, the daughter of Michigan Island Light keeper Edward Lane.

Lane started his career as second assistant at Devils Island in April 1896. A year later he went to Forty Mile Point Light on Lake Huron as first assistant before taking over Michigan Island as keeper in 1902.

His family spent the previous winter of 1901-02 in Detroit. It was common for married keepers from the more remote stations to maintain two households, one of course being the lighthouse and the second someplace in town, either in the nearest community or perhaps close to relatives in another location.

Since her father had to open the light for the early spring shipping season he left Detroit as soon as the ice broke. At the time home life was in a bit of turmoil since all three of his children were sick with whooping cough.[cix] All were under seven so their mother had her hands full. Perhaps feeling overwhelmed and needing to

Edna Lane, the daughter of a Michigan Island lightkeeper, remembers many of the trials and tribulations of being a lightkeeper. Stonehouse Collection

"share" the experience with Edward, her mother packed up the children regardless of their condition and headed north for Michigan Island!

They traveled by train to Chicago and while waiting for the connection at the station, Edna's sister broke out with measles! Since at the time a smallpox epidemic was racing through the city there was some thought the family would be quarantined and prohibited from leaving. Her mother certainly was anxious not to be stranded with three sick children in Chicago, must have done some fast-talking because they managed to grab a train north.

When they finally arrived at Bayfield, Wisconsin, on the late train the conductor helped get them all to a local boarding house where the keepers were staying. Although unstated, the late night arrival must have been a tremendous surprise to Edward!

Edna remembered, "Early the next morning we went on board the *Barker* accompanied by Mrs. Brown, the former keeper's wife. My brother broke out with the measles and my sister, already quite ill, developed pneumonia. When it rains, it pours!

"We landed on the island to find the living quarters a filthy mess. A horsehide had been tacked to the one bedroom floor and the whole place was overrun with roaches. Mom and dad had to scrub everything in order to get the sick ones in bed. From then on it was a struggle to save my sister's life. With the help of the "medicine chest" we all survived. Do you remember the chest? Everything for every known malady with complete directions printed on each bottle. Ours even had chloroform, needles for sewing wounds, etc.

"I remember we felt like aristocrats when our beautiful outhouse, built in Detroit, arrived on the Amaranth–all solid oak inside with a beautiful casement window no less.

"Of course our weekly baths were always taken in a wash tub brought into the kitchen, water heated on the wood burning cook stove. I don't recall whether the water was changed for each bath or whether each of us bathed in the same tub of water. There were times when we had to carry water from the lake for Mom's flower beds and for washing"[cx]

The Luick Women

Being a lightkeeper on a remote Lake Superior island didn't offer much opportunity for social interaction, especially if you were a single man. Stated a little differently, it was a terrible place to meet women!

This was the challenge Emmanuel Luick faced. Born in Cleveland in 1866, by 1892 he was the keeper of the Sand Island Light located on the remote outer fringe of the Apostle Islands. He had worked as a commercial fisherman and wood turner but wasn't satisfied with the employment. Looking for something better, in 1875 he joined the Lighthouse Service becoming an assistant keeper at nearby Outer Island Light. He found lighthouse keeping to his taste. The repetitive nature of the duties, rugged natural beauties of the area and quiet evidently appealed to him. But he was lonely!

While other keepers enjoyed family life, all he had was his own company. He must have longed for a "good woman" to share his life.

Somehow Emmanuel got really lucky, or so he thought, and in the winter of 1896 married beautiful Ella Richardson of Rhode Island. How the two met isn't known. Perhaps she was a mail order bride but this is the wildest speculation. During the summer tourists occasionally visited

Ella and Emmanuel Luick on their marriage.
Stonehouse Collection

the Apostles. They could have met in that fashion. What we do know is that when they married Ella was only 16 years old! Emmanuel was 29 and likely set a bit in the ways of a bachelor.

Young Ella was no shrinking violet, awed by her marriage to an older man or at filling the role of a lightkeeper's wife. While her reaction to being hustled out to live on desolate Sand Island is also a blank, she seemed to adapt well, or at least "toughed it out." The years ground by with winters in a snow bound little town devoid of culture or "civilized" entertainment, not that a keeper's salary allowed for much discretionary spending anyway. The rest of the year wasn't much better, trapped by the cold lake on an isolated hunk of rock! It is too much to conjecture that Ella wanted more; perhaps the excitement of the city, friends visiting and entertaining, an occasional night at the theater or concert! But to be trapped with an old man on a rotten hunk of miserable rock was just too much!

Ella had a different personality than her husband as reflected in the lighthouse log entries. His tended to be short and to the point, making only those official observations directly required by the Lighthouse Service. Ella was far more capricious, willing to let feelings and emotions flood from pen to paper. For example, on August 14, 1899 Emmanuel wrote, *"N.E. breeze and clear cool changed N.E. fresh. Keeper sawed wood till 1 P.M. then went to East Bay with mail but tug failed to come."* As dry as the entry was he might as well have been keeping light in the Sahara! By contrast, Ella wrote on November 23, 1898, *"N.W. very fresh breeze. Thermometer 6 rose to 12 and dropped to 9 above zero. This afternoon Mr. Luick went to the boathouse and brought home from the shanties a pair of 'skees,' belonging to Mr. Louis Moe. He made a poor Norwegian though, but after practicing a while he decided that he could manage them. So he put our four chickens in a bushel basket and the basket in a bag and the 'skees' on his feet and with the bag on his back he started for East Bay. He was home three hours later and says 'skees' are better than walking in 18" of snow, but not as easy as snow shoes."* Clearly this was a couple with two minds and two visions distinctly different!

At the end of the 1901 shipping season Emmanuel became ill and Ella was forced to take over his duties. For three long weeks she kept the light, nursed Emmanuel and handled the required household chores, including preparing to close the station for the winter. It was a backbreaking effort. Several times during her time at the island when she was forced to work in place of her husband the Lighthouse Service officially appointed her as assistant keeper and paid her for the time, but that was rare!

What tension existed in the marriage we can only guess, but on May 19, 1905 she left Emmanuel and the wretched Sand Island Light forever. Emmanuel recorded the sad event in his log with the terse entry, *"Mrs. Ella Luick left for Bayfield on steamer* Barker *at 6PM."* It is interesting to speculate on the anguish that must have gone into Ella's decision to leave and Emmanuel's realization of it. Was it a mutual agreement or strictly Ella's decision? Did she see her life wasting away on lonely Sand Island or a succession of bleak lighthouses as Emmanuel followed his chosen career? Did she yearn for companionship other than her husband's? We know she went to Baltimore but other than that meager clue, all is mystery. In 1906 their divorce was final.

There is some speculation that Ella "fell in" with a local fisherman who was bit of a Romeo around the islands. Being a fisherman meant he had a boat, which for a group of islands was the equivalent of "wheels." He could come and go at will, "seeing" many of the areas' "desperate housewives." Supposedly Ella and the fisherman carried on a clandestine affair with fishing Romeo enticing Ella with promises of a more exciting future only to jilt her when he eventually married another woman. Perhaps depressed over losing her fisherman, Ella fled. That she evidently saw a fisherman as more exciting than her husband is a measure of the quiet desperation she faced and her very limited choices.

Luick spent 16 years at the island and during that period had a dozen assistant keepers, not counting the time Ella held a temporary appointment. Clearly there is the possibility that he was a difficult taskmaster, especially considering seven of the men

Sand Island light must have been a forlorn location for a young woman like Ella. Stonehouse Collection

resigned from the service after having a dose of Luick. Could any of this contributed to Ella's leaving?

Emma Hahn, Emmanuel's niece by his sister, was a frequent visitor to Sand Island. When Ella left she took up residence to keep house and assist where she could. In 1909 she married Walter Daniels, who would spend his career keeping the lights at nearby Devils, Outer and Michigan Islands. Evidently her time on Sand Island acclimated her for the duties of a lightkeepers wife.

Emmanuel married again in 1911 and this time it seems he made a more compatible choice. He and Oramill had four children but sadly only two survived. The first, a girl was born on the lonely island and month later died there. Her bereaved parents buried her on the island.

Emmanuel with his second wife Oramill and child. Stonehouse Collection

Oramill and Emmanuel stayed at Sand Island until 1921 when the light was automated and he transferred to Grand Marais, Minnesota. Interviewed by a reporter from the *Detroit News* in 1931, she provided rare insight to her experiences. "My only neighbors were the wives of fishermen, but we stuck together. We organized a sewing circle and we sewed for the Red Cross and other things. We met twice a month at each other's houses and got up nice little parties, besides. We made much of our birthdays and baked birthday cakes and made the most of what we had.

"We had an 18-foot flat boat with a three-horse power motor and when it was too wet to cross the swampy places, my husband would sometimes run me to a neighbor's in his boat. The soil is not deep on these islands which are mostly sandstone and rocks but some of the fisherman's wives raised some garden stuff and a little fruit. We went three and a half miles for our milk, every other day. Our nearest neighbor was a mile away. The first year we were there Charles Haven was the assistant and he had a wife and two children. Then came Ole Christensen and his wife. At the last there was an unmarried assistant and three of us kept the light. We were six miles from the mainland.

Asked to comment about the change to Grand Marais, she said, "We have had our isolation. Now we are back to civilization."[cxi] All things are certainly relative. Going from a forlorn Apostle Islands lighthouse to Grand Marais and thinking it an improvement is, at best, a reach!

More Lightkeepers

It seems the deeper we dig, the more female lightkeepers come to light (no pun intended). While all have a story to tell, finding it is often a "mission impossible."

Note the large number of wives who replaced deceased husbands. This was virtually the only way a woman could be appointed keeper. There were very few women appointed to the job in their own right. Invariably the only way was for the husband to die "in the saddle" and the wife to be appointed as keeper in sympathy. The attitude was one of the "the poor woman needs a way to provide for herself (family) and the lightkeeper's job is easy enough." The federal government was clearly not an advocate for women.

By the 1920s the Civil Service Commission was actively working to remove women lightkeepers. During the Coast Guard era it too had an active policy of eliminating women from the ranks of keepers. In a 1948 Coast Guard report it was stated, "It was the development of the steam signals and their coal driven boilers and later introduction of heavy duty internal combustion engines, which first placed the duties of lighthouse keepers beyond the capacity of most women. Their gradual retirement from this field of employment was further hastened when intricate electrical equipment was placed at many stations and when the duties of lighthouse keepers gradually came to require special training and when many of the stations were built offshore on submarine foundations. As these changes took place, those women who remained in the lighthouse service were transferred to or were retained at stations where the equipment was of a more simple type."[cxii] Reading between the lines, a woman's place was not in the lighthouse!

Mendota Light was intended to light the way into the Lac La Belle canal. The light was very short lived. Stonehouse Collection

Considering the tremendous contributions women made to the effort to win World War II, from "Rosie the Riveter" to ferrying combat aircraft to working various high technology assembly lines, women were capable of any task a man could do. For the Coast Guard to be able to "get away" with such blatant anti-women rationalization even in 1948 is amazing!

Here are some of the gals we know so little about:

It is said that sometime prior to the erection of the Mendota Light at Bete Gris on Lake Superior, Henrietta Bergh kept an unofficial "light" in the area. Henrietta was a fisherman's wife who fell into the habit of placing a lantern in her upstairs window to help her husband find his way home on dark and stormy nights. While certainly not as effective as a true lighthouse it was far better than empty blackness. According to legend, when other fishermen realized what she was doing, they asked her to always keep it burning for them too! When Mendota Light was first illuminated in 1895, it negated the purpose for Henrietta's light and it burned no more.[cxiii]

Gull Rock Light is a forbidding outpost at the tip of the treacherous Keweenaw Peninsula. Stonehouse Collection

The rear range light also served as quarters for the lightkeeper. Stonehouse
Collection

Alice Nolan was the assistant to her husband John at Gull Rock
Light on Lake Superior from March 1892 to November 1903. Gull
Rock is one of the lonely lights on the tip of the Keweenaw
Peninsula that is often considered at the end of the earth. A husband
and wife team was critical to success at such locations. Earlier, from
September 1872 to July 1877, Mary Cocking served as assistant to
her husband Stephen. When he resigned he was replaced by James
Corgan, whose wife Mary assumed the assistant position.[cxiv]

Mary A. Wheatley kept the Eagle Harbor Range Light on Lake
Superior from 1898 to 1905. The original lighthouse at Eagle
Harbor was established in 1851 and rebuilt in 1870 but without
adequate range lights the harbor was very difficult to enter. The
problem was solved in 1877 with the construction of both front and
rear range lights. The rear range was a simple wood tower showing
a very directional light. The front range light was in a small tower
atop the keeper's quarters. Lining up rear light on top of the front

gave a safe course to bring a vessel down a narrow channel and into the safety of the harbor. When Mary was appointed in June1898 she was the light's first female keeper. She had no family with her and lived alone. When she resigned suddenly at the end of August 1905 Mary Thomson, the wife of the Eagle Harbor Light keeper Thomas, replaced her. Within three weeks he had transferred to the Eagle Harbor range lights and Mary turned over the position to him.[cxv]

Mrs. Julia Griswold kept the Eagle River Lighthouse on Lake Superior from 1861-1865, replacing her husband John Griswold, who as old sailors said, "crossed the bar." John was the first keeper when the light was established in 1859.[cxvi]

Lydia Smith was the assistant keeper of the Manitou Island Light, Lake Superior, 1855-56 while her husband Angus was keeper 1849-1856. A second woman, Mrs. Mary Corgan was the assistant keeper under her husband James from October 1873 until

The front range light was just a small wood tower but it was critically important. Stonehouse Collection

Lonely Granite Island Light helped mark the shipping lane along the south shore of Lake Superior. Stonehouse Collection

his removal in July1875. She and her husband would later serve at nearby Gull Island Light too.[cxvii]

Mrs. Anne Crebassa kept the Sand Point Light (also called the L'Anse Light) on Lake Superior as acting keeper March 29, 1908 to December 5, 1908 upon the death of her husband John.[cxviii]

Annie M. Carlson was an acting assistant keeper of the Granite Island Light on Lake Superior, for nine days in 1905. This lonely two and a half acre island is nothing more than a "hunk of rock." Not one square foot is level. The light became operational in 1868. Located about eight miles north of Marquette and four miles offshore, it is a lonely sentinel for coastal shipping.[cxix]

On December 12, 1861 Marquette, Michigan on Lake Superior, keeper Nelson Truckey was replaced by his wife Eliza. A strong Union man, when the Civil War broke out he helped form Company B, 27th Infantry Regiment, Michigan Volunteers, becoming a second lieutenant for his efforts. He would finish the war as a captain. The unit saw heavy action, participating in some of the most famous campaigns including Vicksburg, the Wilderness, Spotsylvania, The Crater, Petersburg, Cold Harbor and the final pursuit and capture of the traitor Lee at Appomattox Court House in April 1865. When Company B marched off to war, his wife Eliza (Anastasia) took over as keeper. She continued as keeper until October 26, 1865 and was certainly one of the earliest female keepers on the Great Lakes. It can also be argued that because Marquette Light was such an important light for iron ore shipping and the criticality of iron for the Union, Eliza was the most important female keeper in the Great Lakes if not the entire country! While Nelson was keeping faith with the Union, Eliza was keeping faith with the mariners.[cxx]

Mrs. Ella G. Quick kept the Sand Island Light in the Apostle Islands, Lake Superior 1903-06, replacing her husband, Emmanuel Quick on his demise.[cxxi]

At the Mouth of the Detroit River at Gibraltar, Michigan, Mrs. Mary H. Vreeland ran the light from 1876-79, replacing her husband Michael, on his death.[cxxii]

Mamajuda Light in the Detroit River was kept by Mrs. Caroline Litigot (Autaya) from 1874-85 replacing her husband Barney Litigot, on his death. Mamajuda

The 27th Michigan is remembered on the State of Michigan memorial at Vicksburg. Stonehouse Collection

Mamajuda Light was an important aid in the always tricky Detroit River. Stonehouse Collection

Island no longer exists, having mostly washed away in the swift river current. Today it is identified only as "Mamajuda Shoal," with a small cylindrical tower topped with a plastic optic marking the location. Caroline replaced Barney as keeper on January 8, 1874 but was removed on July 1, 1874. Two months later she was "reinstated" serving until July 13, 1876 as Mrs. Caroline Litigot and having married Adolph Antaya, from then until her resignation on May 28, 1885 under Caroline Antaya. Her initial appointment to replace her husband, who was a wounded Civil War veteran, was strictly a sympathy one. His death left her penniless with a family to support. The local inspector objected, claiming she was sick and incompetent and appointed a man to the job. Only intervention of Michigan's U.S. senator to the Secretary of the Lighthouse Board on her behalf restored the appointment to her. Captain Orlo Mason eventually replaced her. The story of his heroic daughter Maebell is told in the original *Women of the Lakes.*[cxxiii]

Mrs. Sarah E. Lane Grand served as acting keeper of the Mission Point Light on Grand Traverse Bay, Lake Michigan 1906-07 following her husband's resignation.

Mrs. William M. Monroe ran the Muskegon Harbor Light on Lake Michigan 1862-71 replacing her husband William Monroe, on his death.

Mrs. Annie McGuire kept the Pentwater Light on Lake Michigan, 1877-85 replacing her husband Francis McGuire, when he "passed." She was reportedly removed in February 1885 for "drunkenness and irregular habits."[cxxiv]

Mrs. Katherine Marvin kept the Squaw Point Light at Little Bay de Noc, Lake Michigan 1898-04, replacing her husband Lemeul, deceased. Squaw Point is just on the other side of Little Bay de Noc from Gladstone, Michigan and was established in 1897 to help guide vessels into that port. Her husband was a wounded Civil War veteran in failing health and doubtless received the appointment in recognition of his service. A small story and a half building with an attached tower it must have been tight quarters for Kate and the four children of her TEN children she still had at home![cxxv]

Mrs. Jane Enos, kept the St. Joseph Light on Lake Michigan, 1876-81, first as the acting keeper when her husband John died in June 1876 and later as keeper from June 1878 until March 1881 when she was removed. Why it took two years to have the "acting" removed is unknown. For roughly three years she had a male assistant keeper, a relative anomaly for a female. She was also not the first female keeper at the light. For a month Mrs. Slatia Carlton was assistant to her husband Monroe Carlton, from November to December 1861.[cxxvi]

Georgia A. Stebbins ran the North Point Light at Milwaukee on Lake Michigan 1881-99, replacing her father D. K. Green. The original light was built in 1838 and in the wrong location, apparently through the normal ineptitude of the lighthouse authorities at the time. In 1854 a new light was constructed atop a tall bluff. Although the light only had a 28-foot tower with a small fourth order Fresnel lens, it had a focal plane of 102 feet and was visible for 14 miles. D. K. Green took over as keeper on September 23, 1871. Two years later his daughter, Georgia Stebbins, who was living in New York City, was diagnosed with consumption and doctors gave her only a short time to live. Georgia's husband had died previously and with nothing to hold her in New York, she traveled to Milwaukee to be with her father. When she arrived in 1874 she found him ill, so she began helping to keep the light. As he grew worse, she grew stronger. Apparently the clean Lake Michigan air was all she needed to restore her health. Gradually she took over more and more of his duties although it was all very unofficial. By the start of the 1881 navigation season he was unable to even give the pretense of keeping the light and since the district superintendent was fully aware of the work Georgia was doing behind the scenes, he arranged for her appointment as acting keeper. Three months later the "acting" was removed and she was a keeper in name as well as fact.

The new light was also in the wrong place since the bluff was eroding faster than expected. One morning she discovered more than 20 feet of it had disappeared during the night! A bare 16 feet separated the tower from the edge of the bluff! The district engineer recommended a new light since any effort to stabilize the bluff was hopeless and moving the light tower was beyond current engineering capability. Work started on a new light in July 1887 and by December a 30-foot tower and two-story Queen Anne style quarters were completed. Georgia moved into the new dwelling and the light was first exhibited on January 10, 1888.

When the light was originally located it was surrounded by wilderness, essentially low value real estate. Over time however, expensive homes were built in the area and it became very "upscale." In 1892 noted landscape architect Frederick Law Olmstead was contracted by Milwaukee to design a 140-acre park encapsulating the new homes as well as lighthouse. The result was named Lake Park. Being part of the scenic park certainly meant Georgia had to pay a bit more attention to the lighthouse grounds than at a more isolated station.

As Milwaukee grew the breakwater lights were improved and since North Light was now partially hidden by vegetation and lost in the glow of city lights, the Lighthouse Service requested Congress decommission it. Congress agreed and on June 30, 1907 it was extinguished and Georgia resigned from the Service. She had been a keeper, paid and unpaid, for 33 years.[cxxvii]

While the Lighthouse Service said the light wasn't needed anymore the mariners disagreed! They claimed it was vital to vessels approaching from the north and pressured to have it relit. To cover for Congressional lethargy, the Milwaukee Chamber of Commerce and Milwaukee Merchants and Manufacturers Association cooperated to run the light as a private aid to navigation. Eventually the light was established in December 1912 but only after building a new tower (the third on the site) which raised the light 154-feet above the lake making it the sixth highest on the Lakes.[cxxviii]

Milwaukee's North Point Light was finally surrounded by a beautiful city park. Stonehouse Collection

Port Washington Light is one of the oldest lights on Lake Michigan.
Stonehouse Collection

Mrs. Schoomer kept the Port Washington Light on Lake Michigan 1860-61, replacing her husband Barnard Schoomer, who went on to a "better world."

Mrs. Eva Pape kept the Sheboygan Light on Lake Michigan 1869-85. Eva was the wife of Louis Pape, a soldier who lost both arms and eyes in the Civil War. Her appointment was strictly out of sympathy although certainly merited.

Mrs. Harry Miller served as assistant keeper at Grand Haven Light October 1872 until the resignation of her husband in September 1875. He was keeper since 1861.

Although not included on the official keepers list, an invoice from the local superintendent of lights requests payment for Mrs. Priscilla Parker for her work keeping the Grand Traverse Point Light from September 11, 1873 to September 30, 1873 at a per diem rate computed on $540 per year. Why she was keeping the light is unknown but since the assigned keeper, Dr. H. Shetterly, died on October 21, 1873, perhaps she was somehow involved in assisting him during his last days. Whether she was ever paid is unknown.[cxxix]

Mary Ryan kept the Calumet Pierhead Light south of Chicago on Lake Michigan from August 7, 1873 until November 18, 1976 as the assistant keeper and from then until October 14, 1880 as the keeper. Why she departed isn't known but her journal entries show clearly that she was not happy with the duties or location. She was assistant keeper to her husband and perhaps his loss and her daily reminder of it was too much to bear.[cxxx]

Mrs. Minnie Hesh Cochems kept the light at Sherwood Point, on Lake Michigan as the assistant for her husband William

Sherwood Point Light was on Green Bay, at the entrance to the Sturgeon Bay Ship Canal. Stonehouse Collection

Cochems. Sherwood Point Light is located on Green Bay, near the west entrance to the Sturgeon Bay Ship Canal. It was reportedly the last manned lighthouse on the Great Lakes. Established in 1883, it was automated a century later. William Cochems was initially assigned to the light as the acting first assistant in 1894 eventually becoming keeper in 1895 on the death of the keeper, Henry Stanley. Minnie became his assistant in 1898 replacing Stanley's wife Katharine who resigned. Minnie remained the assistant until her death in 1928.[cxxxi]

Mrs. Donald E. Harrison ran the St. Marys River Upper Range Light for a month as acting keeper in 1902 before resigning.

Catherine Shook kept the Pointe aux Barques Light, on Lake Huron, 1849-51 following the death of her husband Peter.

Mrs. Anna Garraty ran the Presque Isle Harbor Range Light on Lake Huron, 1903-26, replacing her husband Patrick Garraty, expired. Lightkeeping was a family tradition. Her father Patrick was the keeper at Presque Isle Light when it was first lit in 1871. Her mother Mary was her father's assistant at Presque Isle and three brothers; John (Presque Isle, Detroit River, Devils Island, Mendota, Raspberry Island, Rock of Ages, Stannard's Rock), Patrick Jr. (Middle Island, Presque Isle, St. Clair Flats), and Thomas (Presque Isle, Presque Isle Harbor Range) were keepers.[cxxxii]

Mrs. Julia Brawn was a keeper at the Saginaw River Range Light on Lake Huron 1873-90, replacing her husband, Peter Brawn, stone cold dead. From his death on March 18, 1873 until November 9, 1873. After she married George Way she took a demotion to assistant keeper, which lasted until the job was abolished on October 1, 1882. It is interesting that the assistant keeper position was reestablished the following May and a man, Leonidus Charlton, hired to fill it. George Way died five months later and Charlton resigned the following month. Edward Buzzard was appointed keeper and his wife Nellie the assistant, both would leave in June 1886. There is some question whether the elimination of Julia's position as assistant keeper and subsequent increase in workload for George coupled with the loss of pay was a method of forcing the Ways out of the Lighthouse Service. Circumstantially it would seem so.[cxxxiii]

Mrs. Joanna H. McGee ran the Marblehead Light on Lake Erie 1832-34, replacing her husband George H. McGee, deceased.

Mrs. Ann Edson kept the Turtle Island Light on Lake Erie, 1869-72 replacing her husband Nathan W. Edson, deceased. This small light was established in 1831 at the mouth of the Maumee River and deactivated in 1904 when the Toledo Harbor Light became operational. Records show Ann resigned in September 1872 and was replaced by Samuel Jacobs. Clara Jacobs was listed as the first assistant to her husband from August 1873 through July 1874 when he resigned.[cxxxiv]

CHAPTER SIX

THE RISING SUN

***Rising Sun* Sinks**

A fascinating shipwreck and subsequent "salvation" involves the wrecking of the old steamer *Rising Sun* on October 29, 1917. Not only is the actual disaster worthy of note, but also the circumstances that cause her and the passengers to even exist are nothing short of incredible. The wonderful thing about history is the ability to "connect the dots," to trace the relationships between events, however tenuous. The *Minnie M.* wreck is great example.

The 133-foot steamer was built as the *Minnie M.* in 1884. Her career was long and varied. She ran between Cheboygan and Sault Ste. Marie until 1892, and later from St. Joseph to Chicago. When the Arnold Transit Line, famous for their Mackinac Island ferries, owned her, she ran between the island, Cheboygan and the Soo. Sold to the Algoma Central Railroad, she shifted from the Canadian Soo to Michipicoten. The steamer was an old and well-traveled vessel.

Coupled with the steamer is the story of the Israelite House of David (HOD). This was a (and is) a religious cult established (reestablished?) in Benton Harbor, Michigan in 1903 and in 1916 claimed to have upwards of 1,000 members. As with any cult, there are supporters and detractors. Of late, the cult has been "reinvented" as kind of a quaint collection of longhaired Christian eccentrics. Local apologists would say something like, "Perhaps they are a little strange, but that's' just their way." However in my

The Rising Sun *at the High Island dock. Stonehouse Collection*

opinion, what is behind the public facade is very much darker. The more the bright light of day illuminates the HOD, the more questions arise. What follows is a version of their story that in my opinion is the most accurate. Readers can judge for themselves.

I obviously am not "kind" to the HOD in any regard. I fully consider them to be a cult under any accepted use of the word. "CULT–Any group which has a pyramid type authoritarian leadership structure with all teaching and guidance coming from the person/persons at the top. The group will claim to be the only way to God; Nirvana; Paradise; Ultimate Reality; Full Potential, Way to Happiness etc, and will use thought reform or mind control techniques to gain control and keep their members."[cxxxv] The HOD as well as the other cults I mention certainly meet this definition.

Although the history of HOD is murky, apparently the roots go back to 1620 England when a woman named Joanna Southcott claimed she was the first of the seven messengers that would be sent by God to gather the lost tribes of Israel. One source claims she tried

Photographed as the Algoma, the Rising Sun was a well traveled vessel. Stonehouse Collection

to produce the Second Messenger by "immaculate conception," fell into a deep trance and died in the effort. After her demise, other enterprising entrepreneurs picked up the program moving through messenger two, three, four, five and six. Since the follow on messengers were all male, the rituals of the cult evolved to include outlawing shaving and haircutting. The cult also developed a "cleansing of the blood" ceremony that required the "messenger" to deflower all virgins in the cult prior to their marriage. In Medieval days this was often called the "privilege of the first night" where the local lord had the right to have the new wife spend her wedding night in his bed. In the late 1800s the HOD was forced out of England when the public learned the truth of the unsavory ritual. The cult then separated into three groups, one going to the United States, ending up in Detroit under leader Michael Mills who called himself the Seventh Messenger. This meant he was in today's parlance, "The Man," the final messenger from God with infinite power and authority. Newspapers often called him "Prince Michael." His members gave him as the leader of the cult, all of their property and 100 percent of their earnings.[cxxxvi]

Prince Michael also decreed all the wives would be common property for the men in the group. The men could pass the women around and share them, as they desired, much as a public library loans books. In reaction to the decree, his wife sued for divorce charging adultery and lewd and lascivious cohabitation. Messenger from God or not, there were limits! The newspapers had a field day. In the process of the divorce action not only did she reveal the cult's darkest secrets but also gleefully named each of his "heavenly sent" mistresses! One witness, a 14-year-old girl, claimed he told her, "He was the Son of Man whose special business was to sow good seed for the purpose of purification," certainly a unique pick up line."[cxxxvii] Outraged by the disclosures, a lynch mob formed and authorities filed morals charges against him, especially as it involved the "virgin ritual." One newspaper called him the "Long-Haired Prince of Darkness." Mills was subsequently jailed for five years at Michigan's Jackson State Prison and one of his followers, Benjamin F. Purnell, deftly assumed the leadership of the cult.

Sometimes a cult's created theology can work against it, and this was the case with the HOD. If Mills was the Seventh Messenger as he claimed, then that made Purnell the Eighth Messenger, which of course didn't fit the theology. To work around this problem, Purnell claimed Mills was a fraud and he was the *real* Seventh Messenger! We always have to be leery of fake seventh messengers!

Purnell was the product of the Kentucky hill country, a deep woods backwater over-loaded with religious

The Seventh Messenger, Prince Michael ended up in Jackson Prison. Stonehouse Collection

extremists and miscellaneous meandering mad mullahs. The area is still known for it's out of mid-stream religious leaders. Born in 1861, he also reportedly claimed to be a seventh son, a point of great significance to his followers.[cxxxviii]

Seven is a number rich in biblical associations. There are seven deadly sins, seven Christian virtues, seven petitions in the Lord's prayer; Joshua marched seven times round the walls of the city before flattening them with a blast from seven trumpets on the seventh day of the siege of Jericho, and Pharaoh's dream as

Benjamin and Mary Purnell. Stonehouse Collection

interpreted by Joseph involved seven fat and seven lean cows, seven plump ears of corn and seven blighted ones. In general folklore mystery also attaches to the number seven; magical properties are attributed to seventh sons and seventh sons of seventh sons. The power of the number seven stretches far back in time: around 2500 BC a great Sumerian king built a temple in the city of Adab to the goddess Nintu, with seven gates and seven doors, purified with the sacrifice of seven times seven fatted oxen and sheep. Antiquarians found many reasons to see the number seven as especially important.[cxxxix]

HOD followers believed Jesus Christ was the First Coming and his purpose was saving souls. The Second Coming, or Shiloh, the Seventh Messenger as foretold in Revelations, was the "Ingathering" when the twelve lost tribes of Israel, 144,000 people, would assemble. Christ would return for the Second Coming and the adherents would receive salvation of body as well as soul. In other words, the HOD believed the physical body would be saved in addition to the soul. Traditional Christian groups believed in the immortality of the soul but not the body. As the Seventh Messenger, Purnell was in effect Christ's personal agent.

HOD didn't emerge from a vacuum. While it clearly is a different group, it was not unique in terms of being a Christian based cult. This period of American History was rich in the number and variety of strange and wondrous mystical groups that sprang forth from the fertile brains of self-serving leaders. The religious landscape was (and is) populated by a magical myriad of cults including:

The Devine Science and Unity School cult started in 1889. By the 1920s it was immensely success-ful selling salvation by mail in plain brown wrappers.

Mary Baker Eddy, born in New Hamp-shire in 1821, found-ed the First Church of Christ, Scientist (Christian Science) in 1879. The move-ment grew to an estimated 270,000 members by 1936 although today it is estimated at less than 100,000. Considered by some to be a mere

Mary Baker Eddy. Stonehouse Collection

confidence scam, Eddy was soon charging pupils $300 for instruction in the cult's teachings. An entire line of various religious products enhanced the organization's bottom line.[cxl] When Eddy finally "assumed ambient temperature,"[cxli] followers eagerly waited her reincarnation. That she did not rise again failed to dampen their enthusiasm. Many followers considered her the equivalent of Christ so the delay must be divinely inspired and therefore excusable. The "church" continues today!

Starting in 1850, the Brotherhood of New Life," spewed a collage of sexually mystical beliefs and practices focusing in part on "divine spirits," all in the scheme of communal living. Adherents were supposed to copulate with the spirits, begetting spiritual children. Although members were to be celibate in this world, stories circulated of orgies, nudity, wife swapping and the like.[cxlii]

Although there is some confusion regarding their origin the Jehovah's Witness cult emerged from the shadows in the 1870s. Under the leadership of Charles Taze Russell, it soon became a growing movement. Russell's identification as a confidence man failed to diminish follower's eager enthusiasm for the cult.[cxliii]

Jehovah's Witnesses draw their roots from a Nineteenth Century American Adventist movement. One William Miller, a Baptist

Charles Taze Russell made the Jehovahs Witnesses a major force. Stonehouse Collection

preacher, began forecasting in 1816 that the "end was near" and Christ would return to earth in 1843. The attraction of this "Second Advent" captured the hearts and minds of thousands of people who eagerly awaited the return. When it failed to happen on schedule, Miller recalculated and announced it was really March 1844. When this prediction failed also, his movement greatly diminished but small groups of die-hards still remained loyal and continued to recalculate the return. One group evolved into the Seventh Day Adventists, a variant becoming the Jehovah's Witnesses (JW). The official

William Miller often forecasted the return of Christ. Stonehouse Collection

JW line however claims direct descent from the beginning of the Bible. Of course in my opinion, this is so much rhetorical nonsense. Another splinter group evolved into the infamous Branch Davidian cult that David Koresh led to a fiery death in Waco, Texas in 1993.[cxliv] The foolish leading the gullible begat the confused.

The group has used numerous names; Watch Tower Bible and Tract Society, Zion's Watch Tower, Millennial Dawn, People's Pulpit Society Association, The Brooklyn Tabernacle, International Bible Students Association among others. Changing the name frequently created confusion among the world at large and helped hide the group from scrutiny. They also changed their doctrine too! One source claims between 1917 and 1928 it changed 148 times![cxlv]

All failed prophecies aside the JWs are an amazingly successful cult. In 2000 they claimed a worldwide membership of over 6 million in 91,000 congregations! They recruit very heavily, claiming they are the only Christian religion on earth. All of the others are false.[cxlvi] JWs are supposed to spend five hours a week doing door to door "visitation" of non-members and sell 12 subscriptions to the *Watchtower* (the cult newspaper) a month. The *Watchtower* however has an amazingly bad record as a predictor, having forecast the end of the world for 1914, 1918, 1925, 1975 and 1989. Predicting the end of the world is one thing, having people actually believe such foolishness is another. Many JWs placed enough faith in the paper, they sold their homes, quit jobs, etc. to await their delivery to heaven! Doubtless they were disappointed when the promised event failed to occur and the old earth continued to spin merrily on its axis through the universe![cxlvii]

His family always claimed Joseph Smith, the developer of Mormonism, had a very active imagination. Library of Congress

Certainly the most successful of the cults was (and is) that of the Mormons or "Church of Jesus Christ of the Latter Day Saints." Today an estimated two million members world wide claim to belong and the group dominates the life of an entire U.S. state and greatly influences the surrounding area. Although far more successful than the HOD, there are eerie similarities.

In my opinion there are two ways to look at Mormonism. One view is that old Joe Smith was an absolute fraud and his created religion is just so much nonsense intended to swindle the terminally gullible. If however you are a Mormon, then Joe and his scribbled scripture is the best thing since sliced bread, canned beer and colored prophylactics. It is all in the point of view. If you believe, you believe.

Joseph Smith, Jr founded the cult. Although he was born to a poor family in Vermont in 1805, his family later immigrated to western New York. In 1820, at the age of 14, he claimed both God and Jesus visited him, telling him all the accepted churches were wrong and he should steer clear of them. Three years later Smith claimed the angel Moroni came calling and told him of a secret cache of mysterious gold plates that related the story of the ancient inhabitants of North America.[cxlviii] Because the plates' inscription was in an unknown language, claimed later to be "Reformed Egyptian," two mystical stones, Urim and Thummin, were conveniently buried with the plates to aid in the translation.[cxlix] Four years later the location of the extraordinary plates and magic rocks are mystically revealed to Smith. Shovel in hand, Smith heads out to the woods and digs up his treasure! Of course Smith is alone when he unearths the plates, other than his wife Emma who he instructs to turn her back so she couldn't see him work. Cult leaders are always very trustworthy so don't question them on such actions. Using the magic stones, Smith labors for three long years before he is finally able to finish translating the script. The result is the *Book of Mormon*.

Once his new religion took off, Smith took the title, "Prophet, Seer and Revelator" and claimed he alone spoke with God.

Smith's death threw the cult into turmoil. He was the visionary, the leader! Who could replace him as a host to the various visiting "visions? The leadership struggle was difficult with numerous men (never women) asserting their right to the divine throne. Eventually Brigham Young brokered enough support form cult elders to take the leadership role. Those on the out, split away to form their own operations. For example, Elder James Jesse Strang would eventually end up on Beaver Island on Lake Michigan with a group of approximately 2,000 followers, Smith's brother William among them. Strang reportedly had a personal letter from Smith appointing him successor in the event of Smith's death. Since the letter cut Brigham Young out of the crown, he denounced it as a forgery. If it was accepted as genuine, all of Young's work toiling in Smith's shadow was wasted. Thus Young moved quick and hard to squash any competitors.

Scholars who examined the *Book of Mormon* found it heavily plagiarized the *King James Bible* and its close discussion of contemporary (1820) New York political issues was ludicrous in view of its claims to be the translation of an inscription reportedly thousands of years old.[cl] Good document forgery is very hard to accomplish.[cli] Faking historical documents is especially difficult since facts; styles and material can be cross-checked with other sources. Religious documents are far easier to phony up since people tend to "believe" in them, regardless of the "facts." Such is true of the *Book of*

Brigham Young took the leadership of the Mormon movement after an internal struggle with church elders. Library of Congress

Mormon, perhaps, in my opinion, the largest hoax ever promulgated on the human race.

There are numerous sub cults to the main Mormon cult. The Fundamentalist Church of Jesus Christ of Latter Day Saints, based in Utah and Arizona, recently opened a new "retreat" in El Dorado, Texas, much to the chagrin of local residents. This is thought to be the largest polygamist faction in the country, with an estimated 10,000 members. Another retreat is in British Columbia. The cult openly promotes polygamy and has been accused of forced marriages, welfare system abuse and wife swapping. Like other cults, the public face is benign and private activity entirely different.[clii]

In sum the Mormon movement well illustrates not only the tremendous imagination of Joseph Smith to be able to develop such a unique and far fetched package of nonsense, but more important, his incredible ability to sell it to others. If, as old P.T. Barnum said, "There is sucker born every minute," Utah must be the most gullibility capital of the world! The similarity with the HOD is eerie.

The Shakers were another American cult that expanded greatly in the 1840s having perhaps 6,000 members in 19 communities. As numbers increased, so did the public scrutiny with charges of being anti-Christian common. Critics claimed their rituals were blasphemy and the near worship of founder Mother Ann Lee evil. Families that joined lost control of their children and extreme physical punishment was common. Members who escaped the confines of the cult claimed the leaders drank alcohol (in violation of the rules), exploited women sexually and lived fat on the work of ordinary members.[cliii]

Spiritualists like the infamous Fox sisters duped weak-minded believers for years with tricks supposedly proving contact with the "other world." The spirits of Napoleon and Abraham Lincoln were said to be regular visitors to the Fox sisters' parlor. From 1848-88 the three sisters claimed they could communicate with the dead. When they finally admitted it was all nothing but simple parlor tricks, supporters continued to believe. "Don't confuse us with fact! We believe!" During the same period spiritualist Helena Blavatsky claimed to have discovered the secrets of long forgotten Tibetan temples allowing her entrance to the "world beyond." Regardless of periodic scandals and exposes of classic medium tricks, a loyal band of followers swore by her "gift."

In my opinion, the Church of Scientology is a modern example of the old song of gullibility. In its May 6, 1991 issue, *Time Magazine* stated, "Scientology poses as a religion but really is a ruthless global scam" and that it "was a hugely profitable global racket."

The infamous Fox sisters duped the public for years. Library of Congress

The cult was started in 1953 by one L. Ron Hubbard, science fiction writer specializing in self-help rackets. When his book *Dianetics* had pretty well run course in terms of sales, he converted it into a religion. The cult stresses using celebrity members as a way of attracting the common folk to the fold. Although it has been in constant trouble with the Federal government because of its scam actions, there are still those who "believe."[cliv]

It focuses on "unhappy" people and promises to make their lives better. It advertises its books often on TV giving the impression they are "best sellers." The reality is such "best seller" status is reached only when supporters buy them by the armload, 50 to 200 copies at a crack.[clv]

Clearly I take a dim view of all religious cults. Certainly people have every right to private religious beliefs and organizations: worship the tooth fairy if you want! However, at such point that cult beliefs and practices damage innocent victims (abuse of children, women and denial of basic human rights, denial of free will by mind control, failing to treat human life with dignity or respect, etc.) then society at large needs to have a full understanding of the true nature of the cult, not just the public relations babble the groups promulgate. Ask yourself why the cults hide their actions and "worship" activities from nonmembers, take offense when criticized etc. While critiquing religious beliefs is currently "politically incorrect" the ones I have discussed are not only in "left field" but also really "out of the ball park."

So why do I open this Pandora's box anyway? What do the various cults have to do with Great Lakes women and their maritime involvement?

First of all, why did these cults come into being, all roughly at the same time? Theologians offer many different explanations. Perhaps a general turning away from conventional Judeo-Christian churches is the simplest explanation. It was an extremely dynamic period in American history. Old orders were crumbling, new inventions were popping up daily and the wonders of science promised all answers to all problems. New political freedoms meant more options for everyone. While conventional religions provided a stable rock for the future, fringe elements of society looked for ways to break away. Since all religion is essentially belief and not "proof" based, any good charismatic salesmen could invent a religion overnight and with perseverance and luck, recruit enough followers to grow profitable. And so the Mormons, JWs, etc... and HOD arrived on the American scene.

Like other cults, the HOD practiced a clear and systematic abuse of women. That so many women (including Great Lakes women) seemingly accepted the subjugation as part of God's order is difficult to understand.

As King Strang's Mormon colony was on Beaver Island, King Purnell's HOD High Island harem was just a few miles to the west. What was there about this corner of Lake Michigan that attracted such weirdness? Is there some kind of "cosmic force" involved, perhaps a tear in the space-time continuum? Perhaps this could become the basis for a new religion? In any case, we have detoured enough into the world of cults.

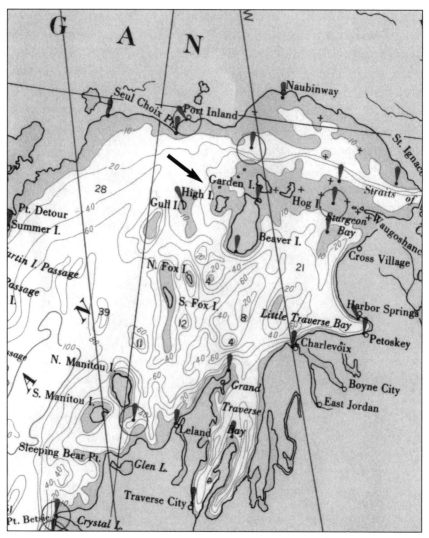

Many of the HOD flock agreed with Purnells' self-serving interpretation of becoming the new Seventh Messenger and migrated with him to Fostoria, Ohio. At this point, he slips off into the "deep end" of the pool, cutting his red hair and beard to resemble the classic Christian image of Christ (remember since no one ever recorded Christ's actual image during his life time, artist renditions are at best, wild guesses). He also claimed he was Christ's younger brother (very much younger!) When his daughter

Hettie was killed in an explosion in a fireworks factory in 1903 and he refused to "raise her from the dead," many locals realized he wasn't quite the messiah he claimed and left him. He and his remaining flock then drifted to Benton Harbor, Michigan. Remember, a basic tenet of the faith was the profession of eternal life of the body as well as soul. Hettie's failure to "arise" was disastrous to Purnell's followers. Under the teachings of the cult, death showed a weakness of the faith. Not only were the dead, dead but also they were obviously sinful since they would not have died in the first place, or at least quickly arise!

Supposedly Benton Harbor was selected because his wife Mary had a "divine inspiration." Perhaps the availability of good land at cheap prices was part of the inspiration, as well as a rural location far from prying eyes! Remember cults do not thrive under close scrutiny, so the more isolated the better. Mary was Purnell's second wife. He deserted his first wife and six month old daughter earlier.[clvi] Important cult leaders like Purnell are not bound by the normal obligations of marriage. He changed the name of the group to the Israelite HOD too, but it was usually just called the HOD.

Purnell was an active recruiter. Setting on top of a pyramid meant the more people he added to the bottom, the higher he soared to the heavens. Considering the people joining the cult surrendered all of their possessions to Purnell, the richer and more powerful he became. Specially trained HOD recruiters were dispatched across the country and world to find more members of the "lost tribes" to swell the ranks of the faithful. A group of 85 Australians joined in 1905 and it wasn't unusual for groups of 10-15 to arrive at the colony.[clvii]

As more and more members of the lost tribes arrived at sleepy little Benton Harbor local residents certainly wondered what kind of strange people were in their midst. Newspapers soon called the leaders of the longhaired colony "King Ben" and "Queen Mary" although within the colony they were just known as Brother Benjamin and Sister Mary. They did wield great power among their followers and increasingly more economic power within the local non-HOD community. Like any good cult leader, Purnell maintained control through veiled threats of deadly force, favored positions and rewards, excommunication or exile. They also practiced communal living, vegetarianism, did not drink alcoholic beverages, use tobacco or cut their hair or beard. Even in a rural area like Benton Harbor, the HOD stood out as a group that didn't belong to conventional society.

It is claimed that over the next nearly quarter of a century, Purnell built a personal fortune of $10 million. The cult (or Purnell depending on one's outlook), owned lucrative farms, a beer garden, (remember, although they couldn't consume alcohol, they could brew and sell it, how's that for a double standard?) factories, buildings, a village of 900 people, traveling baseball teams and a very popular amusement park. Eden Springs Park built in 1908, was considered a premiere tourist attraction in the Mid-West, with buses bringing visitors from the Pere Marquette railroad station and Lake Michigan docks. Chicago was only a short 60 miles across the lake, a quick four or five hour run for the big excursion steamers. Arcade games, a zoo, free stage entertainment and a passenger carrying miniature railroad train captivated hordes of visitors. The park provided employment for HOD members and perhaps more important, earned a substantial cash income necessary for cult operations. The cult also operated a successful fruit packing company and mill operation, auto dealership, motel, nightclub and hospital.

The House of David baseball team was nationally known. Stonehouse Collection

Although unlike the Mormon cult leader King James Jesse Strang of Beaver Island, Purnell never had himself crowned King of his flock, it can be argued his followers were virtual slaves, required to wear cheap clothes, could not own anything of real value, use tobacco or alcohol, eat meat or have public displays of affection. Marriages were performed in mass ceremonies, but of course only after the required "deflowering of the virgins" by the Seventh Messenger. Purnell arranged marriages; they were never by chance. Love or even mutual affection was not part of the process. In a strange contradiction of theology (or perhaps not so strange if the opportunities offered to the Seventh Messenger's harem is considered), cult members were required to practice celibacy, which tended to severely limit internal growth.

Innovative, the cult is credited with inventing the automatic pinsetter for bowling alleys. Seventeen years before the 19th Amendment to the U.S. Constitution gave females the right to vote, the HOD reputedly allowed their full participation in cult affairs, which begs the question of why the women took such a subservient role generally.

The HOD is perhaps most remembered for its very successful barnstorming baseball teams. Purnell knew the power of good publicity and since baseball was the great American pastime, HOD teams were excellent advertising and

James Jesse Strang ran another religious cult on nearby Beaver Island. Is there something in the area to attract such fringe groups. Stonehouse Collection

an efficient method to deflect public attention from the darker side of the cult. Not only did the teams earn money, they also helped recruit new members for the HOD. With the players sporting long flowing beards, they combined solid baseball skills with Harlem Globetrotter style play. The top rated team traveled the United States, Canada, Mexico and Europe playing in various exhibitions and advertising the glories of the HOD. There was even a girl's team, which reportedly was never defeated.[clviii] It was claimed in 1933 a HOD team defeated the St. Louis Cardinals in an exhibition game. The HOD starting pitcher for the game, who only threw one inning, was Jackie Mitchell, supposedly the first female player in professional baseball.[clix] A 3,500-seat stadium in Benton Harbor served as their "home" field. When the HOD began to crumble it was harder and harder to find genuine HOD players and the cult resorted to a little skullduggery. When they were exposed for using paid professionals in wigs and fake beards, the baseball gimmick folded.

The law finally caught up to Purnell however and a bucket of moral charges were registered against him starting in 1910. One of his later accusers claimed Purnell had, "sexual intercourse with about all of the girls of the colony over the age of 12 years. He would take all the girls to his room… quote scripture… and (tell us) he was purified and had the right to have intercourse with any girl of the colony. He would take the girls out of the room into his private room one at a time and bring them back. He would go to the girls' room (in a separate building constructed as a girls dormitory–author's comment) where there were four girls to a room and have intercourse with one girl while the others were all there. I saw that myself. He has all kinds of intoxicating liquors there which he gives to the girls."[clx]

Another female accused him of keeping a harem of 30-50 girls between 13-15 years of age and that he seduced and raped between 200-500 girls under religious pretext."[clxi] A different woman testified that Purnell had sexual relations with her since age 15 and to keep her from testifying against him, he forced her into marriage with a man she did not know, thus "explaining" her "non-virginal" condition. Even though she was married, she claimed he still brought her to the mansion to "use" her as he wanted.[clxii]

Purnell had a long history of such morals problems. As early as 1896, a woman filed a charge of immoral conduct against him. Five years later he was reputedly caught "in the act," with a farmer's wife in an Ohio berry patch.[clxiii] Apparently the charges did not result in penal action, but likely the itinerate preacher did quickly "itinerate" out of town! Whether other charges were made in other rural locations are unknown. Considering the social stigma such charges reflected on their chargers, it is (the author's opinion) likely many were not publicized.

Accusations against Purnell had swirled about for 20 years or so but the cult leader was able to play "rope-a-dope" with them. Mostly the charges were apparently hurled by disgruntled former members. A member could leave anytime but the worldly goods previously handed over to the HOD when they entered remained. The seeds for discontent were clear. By claiming the accusers had strong motives to speak ill of HOD and hiding the true nature of the cult, Purnell continued without hindrance.

While Purnell's followers toiled hard for their daily bread, lived in shacks and dormitories and wore rough and simple clothing, he and his wife lived in high style. His mansion was large, spacious and well furnished as befitting a successful business leader. The building was often called "Diamond House" because of glittering hematite ore mixed into the cement blocks forming the structure. Purnell always wore a sharp looking white suit and flashy jewelry and with his Christ-like hair and beard, cut a remarkable figure. Purnell often traveled about his colony to inspect daily activities, often accompanied by a group of gorgeous young girls. Detractors doubtless claimed, "Where there is smoke, there is fire," and there was lots of smoke around the HOD.

When the *Detroit Free Press* ran a series of sensational investigative stories on the HOD in 1923, the State Attorney General was finally forced into action, filing such charges as rape, statutory rape, religious fraud, and managing a commune that was a public nuisance, prostitution, bigamy, perverse sex, religious imposter, teaching perjury, forcing marriage and others. Raids against the colony followed but Purnell could not be found. For four long years he simply disappeared! It was thought he fled to Canada or even Australia. Sighting reports flowed in from every corner of the U.S. fueled doubtlessly by a State reward of $3,000 and an additional $1,000 "sweetener" by the *Detroit Free Press*. Everyone wanted Purnell. Eventually a disgruntled female follower "squealed" to the police and the elusive Seventh Messenger was discovered hiding in a secret room deep in his mansion. The woman was a victim of his "cleansing" and knew his darkest secrets. When police, accompanied by reporters, burst in to the hidden chamber, it was said Purnell was discovered in bed with a bevy of virgins anxious to be virgins no more. Various legal actions followed. After a sensational trial filled with revelations and titillating testimony from a bevy of beauteous babes, both Purnell and his wife were eventually found guilty of religious fraud while the other charges were not pursued. The intention of the State was to put Purnell out of business. Charges beyond that goal were superfluous. As a result the court fight, HOD was placed in receivership. The Purnells appealed but the court upheld the conviction, finding Purnell guilty of the, "most disquieting crimes against young girls."[clxiv] Woman after woman repeated similar stories of debauchery. The HOD defense lawyers claimed the women were all part of a vast (right wing?) conspiracy against the good, honorable, pure as the driven snow, messenger from God (just ask him if you have doubts), Purnell. What his long-suffering wife Mary must have thought of Purnell's official cleansing duties is unknown. Some stories claim she left the mansion in response to his predilection for young girls. Leaving the cult was out of the question. There was too much at stake economically. No one ever suggested she took male "disciples" but the mind does wander in that direction.

Eventually the Michigan Supreme Court overturned the verdicts on a technicality but after the harsh light of the trial, the power of the HOD was in decline. Purnell died of diabetes and tuberculosis shortly after the legal battling ended. Those members who hadn't fled during the sordid realities of the trial revelation, held a tearful vigil over the body waiting for Purnell to awake! For three days the faithful kept the body warm with hot water bottles.^{clxv} Only on the fourth day when it began to stink with rot was it sent to a funeral home for embalming. Local legend says it was returned to the mansion where it remains in a glass-topped coffin hidden deep in secret burial vault, waiting patiently for physical resurrection.

Cults do not die easily however, and shortly after his death, his wife Mary suddenly discovered that she was *really* the Seventh Messenger and tried to reorganize the followers that remained. (Cross my heart and hope to die if I ain't the Messenger.") Many had left when the trial revealed the cult's "house of cards." When the dust settled Mary and half of the members still remaining, roughly 200 became "Mary's City of David" (MCOD) and moved to other property. The remainder stayed with the HOD accountant, H.T. Dewhirst, on the original grounds. The court split the assets equally between the two groups. For a time both cults chugged along, the conditioned (brainwashed) members doing what they always did. Crowds still came to the amusement park in enough numbers to justify operation until it shut down in the 1960s after a long decline. Various other HOD enterprises continued until they too just ran out of steam, victims of the split, changes in public values and a dying vision. Mary died in 1953 at age 91. The two groups still exist in the Benton Harbor area but in vastly reduced numbers, HOD having four members and MCOD, seven.^{clxvi}

All of this is background for the *Rising Sun* wreck. Before the whole scheme exploded, in 1912 the HOD purchased the lumber rights to about 3,500 acres of High Island, located just to the west of Beaver Island, off the northwest coast of Michigan's Lower Peninsula. To harvest the timber, HOD established a lumber camp and related operation on the island, which necessitated a steamer to haul workers and product back and forth. To meet this need in 1913 HOD purchased the *Minnie M.* to handle the job, renaming her the *Rising Sun.*

The name supposedly came from the mythology of the cult. It was claimed Benjamin and Mary Purnell spent seven years as itinerant preachers wandering through Indiana, Kentucky and Ohio before settling for a time at a farm in Fostoria, Ohio, near the village of Rising Sun. Symbolism for such a movement is always important, thus resurrecting the name sends a powerful message.

The HOD also raised a considerable amount of vegetables on High Island, including cabbage, carrots and potatoes. Since the HOD practiced vegetarianism, exploiting the rich fishing grounds around the island was not part of the economic plan. Infrastructure on the island included a blacksmith shop, bakery, homes, bunkhouses, various roads and a large dock. At the height of the HOD activity on the island, roughly 130 cult members were "ashore."

Some sources claim High Island was used as a place to hide women away during various morals investigations, especially during the infamous trial following the *Detroit Free Press* expose in 1923. Two years earlier an octagonal structure called the "Round House" with eight pie-shaped bedrooms was built to house 16 women who wintered on the lonely island. HOD claimed the women were workers from Eden Park who "earned" the trip as a reward for hard work. This explanation defies logic. Why anyone would want to spend the winter in a drafty cabin without facilities on a remote inhospitable island is ludicrous. Some islanders called it the "house of virgins" The State claimed they were sent there to prevent their testimony. One newspaper called it the "Siberia of America."

Stories claimed cult troublemakers were shipped to the island, regardless of sex and that the shoreline was strewn with the bones of the banished. Others were certain the dead were buried in unmarked graves. The most sensational tales involved a harem kept on the island by Purnell. To a point, many believed the tales, including some HOD members. A male follower quickly deserted the cult when he was ordered to the island. He had heard too many stories to end up there if he could avoid it![clxvii]

One of the High Island women testified she was sent with 29 other girls to the island when the morals trial activity grew too hot.

By going to the island, the girls were considered beyond the reach of a court subpoena to testify. While at the island the girls were also told they had to choose a husband. If they failed to select one, they would remain stranded on the island indefinitely. No husband, no freedom. The girls quickly made their decisions to either select a mate or defy Purnell. Surprisingly all of them, including the few who defied Purnell and did not pick a mate were loaded on the steamer. When the *Rising Sun* reached the dock at South Haven the captain was given a telegram instructing him to "unload the green timber at South Haven" and the "dry timber at Benton Harbor." It was later claimed "green timber" referred to young and unmarried girls and "dry timber" to older or married women. The "green timber" girls went quickly by automobiles to Benton Harbor for a mass wedding to their hastily selected grooms. The "dry timber" was safely "put in the barn."[clxviii] It could be assumed a "cleansing" ceremony would precede the weddings.

When the state prosecutor finally brought charges against Purnell he specifically included High Island, claiming members were, "virtually imprisoned and marooned upon the holdings of said colony on ...High Island in Lake Michigan...that the worse defectives of said colony under a virtual decree of banishment are sequestered on said island without home, school life or the privileges of civic society, the children on the island are reared as primitive aborigines and virtual outcasts of society with no opportunity for betterment..."[clxix]

On the afternoon of October 29, 1917, the *Rising Sun* left High Island bound for St. Joseph. Aboard was a cargo of lumber, produce from the island farm, 18 crewmen and 14 passengers, most young schoolgirls. Specifically why the girls were aboard isn't known. Were they heading to Benton Harbor for a mass wedding or returning from some kind of banishment or religious retreat? Shortly before departure a storm began to blow and the captain thought it better to be on the lake rather than moored to his very unsheltered dock. The steamer hadn't gone far when the storm increased in fury and thick snow showers blotted out visibility.

The girl's band serenades King Ben in his mansion. Stonehouse Collection

Using only dead reckoning, the steamer worked her way into the dreaded Manitou Passage, between the mainland and North and South Manitou Islands.[clxx] In effect he was running blind in one of the most dangerous areas on Lake Michigan.

Shortly before 10:00 p.m. the steamer bounced over rocks off Pyramid Point, on the mainland, approximately 50 miles south of High Island and eight miles north of Sleeping Bear Point. His dead reckoning calculations ran him too far east! The rocks stripped away both rudder and propeller. The *Rising Sun* was helpless and at the mercy of an unmerciful storm. Driven broadside to the seas, the old steamer soon fetched up on a sandbar a couple of hundred feet offshore. With the steamer breaking up underneath him, the captain ordered, "abandon ship."

Fortunately she had five lifeboats so there was plenty of lifesaving capacity. He ordered the first boat ashore with a crew of young men feeling they could assist as additional boats reached the beach. The first boat safely reached the sandy shore, the powerful waves driving it quickly through the surf. The second one, loaded with HOD "schoolgirls" capsized in the surf, throwing them all into the freezing water amid their helpless screams, the men rushed into

The old schooner Rosa belle *replaced the* Rising Sun. *The schooner was lost on Lake Michigan in 1921 with all hands under mysterious circumstances. Stonehouse Collection*

the waves and dragged all to safety. The combination of such a fierce storm ridden out in a relatively small vessel with monstrous waves and screaming winds, rolling and pitching in such desperate conditions while blinded by driving snow, must have been terrifying for the young girls. Likely most were seasick, wishing perhaps for death rather than life. Once on the beach, it was cold, wet and thoroughly miserable, but each boat, assisted by those ashore, made it past the dangerous breakers to safety.

Some of the men went up the beach and found shelter at the home of a local resident. The Glen Haven Coast Guard Station also participated the following day by pulling the last man off the vessel. Somehow he was missed in the general confusion of the shipwreck. The vessel later went to pieces in the waves.

The HOD had poor luck with vessels. In 1910 they lost the small scow-schooner *Emily and Eliza* in Platte Bay, near Sleeping Bear.[clxxi] After the *Rising Sun* wrecked, they acquired the old two-masted schooner *Rosa Belle*. Built in 1863, she was another hard luck boat, lost on Lake Michigan in 1921 with all hands (somewhere between 10-28 souls) under mysterious circumstances.[clxxii] The capsized hull was found floating 40 miles east of Milwaukee on Halloween eve. Her stern was ripped off. Based on several reported incidents with the Lake Michigan carferries, some HOD members believed she was purposely run down in mid lake.

No cult tale is complete without a treasure story. One popular book on hidden and lost treasures claims $11 million is secreted in or near the HOD's Benton Harbor Diamond House. There were other claims of concealed treasure following Purnell's death. Reportedly a stash of more than $120,000 was secreted somewhere deep in the mansion. One story claimed a family turned over $100,000 in cash to Purnell before joining the cult. Where did the money go? Tales of bushel baskets filled with five and ten dollar gold pieces and precious jewels only add spice to the HOD legend. If Purnell ever thought he might have to "cut and run" quickly to escape from the law, having a ready bag of money around was important.[clxxiii]

In the end it all comes down to the question, "What is it about the Beaver Island area of Lake Michigan that so attracts the likes of Purnell and Strang, and the women that so eagerly followed them?" Great Lakes women were usually made up of sterner stuff than those "captured" by the cults.

ENDNOTES/FOOTNOTES

[i] *Detroit Free Press*, April 21, 1874

[ii] Stonehouse Collection, *Marine City* file.

[iii] Patrick Folkes, "Cooks and Ladies' Maids: Women in Sail and Steam on the Great Lakes in the Nineteenth Century." *Freshwater* (Volume 1, Number 1, Spring 1986), p.24.

[iv] *British Whig* Folkes, p. 25.

[v] August 19, 1880.

[vi] *Globe*, December 8, 1882.

[vii] *Oswego Palladium*, April 15, 1872

[viii] http://www.boatnerd.com; *St. Joseph Evening Herald*, September 13, 1902; Stonehouse Collection–Experiment

[ix] http://www.boatnerd.com; *St. Joseph Traveler*, July 13, 1859; Stonehouse Collection–Sunshine

[x] *Detroit Free Press*, October 30, 1906

[xi] *Annual Report, U. S. Life-Saving Service*, 1906, p. 107.

[xii] *Detroit Free Press*, November 11, 1890; http://www.boatnerd.com/Swayze/Bruno.

[xiii] *Duluth Herald*, September 15, 1915; Stonehouse Collection–Onoko.

[xiv] Stonehouse Collection–Whip

[xv] Stonehouse Collection, *Hattie Wells*

[xvi] Stonehouse Collection–Hurricane

[xvii] *Annual Report, U.S. Life-Saving Service*, 1881.

[xviii] Imprecations–"to invoke evil upon, to utter curses"

[xix] *Annual Report, U.S. Life-Saving Service*, 1881.

[xx] Stonehouse Collection, *Hartzell* file

[xxi] Different sources give different dates, to include April 11 or 23 and different numbers of passengers and crew, 4, 9 and 10 being commonly used.

[xxii] Stonehouse File–*Arcadia*; http://www.boatnerd.com/Swayze/Arcadia

[xxiii] Stonehouse Collection–*Dean Richmond*;

[xxiv] http://www.boatnerd.com/Swayze/C.O.D.

[xxv] *Kingston Chronicle and Gazette*, November 27, 1839.

xxvi *Detroit Free Press*, July 7, 1890.

xxvii George W. Hilton, Eastland, *Legacy of the* Titanic (Sanford, California: Stanford University Press, 1995) pp. 284-308.

xxviii Stonehouse Collection, *Eastland* file.

xxix *Chicago Tribune*, July 26, 1915.

xxx *Chicago Tribune*, July 26, 1915; http://www.eastlanddisaster.org.

xxxi *Chicago Tribune*, July 26, 1915.

xxxii *Chicago Tribune*, July 26, 1915.

xxxiii *Chicago Tribune*, July 26, 1915.

xxxiv *Chicago Tribune*, July 26, 1915

xxxv *Chicago Tribune*, July 26, 1915

xxxvi *Chicago Tribune*, July 26, 1915

xxxvii *Chicago Tribune*, July 25, 1915

xxxviii *Chicago Tribune*, July 25, 1915

xxxix *Chicago Tribune*, July 25, 1915

xl *Chicago Tribune*, July 25, 1915.

xli *Chicago Tribune*, July 25, 1915.

xlii *Chicago Tribune*, July 25, 1915.

xliii Dennis R. Duncan, Jr., "Indiana's Deadliest Shipwreck, the *Material Service*," *Inland Seas* (summer 2004), pp. 119-118; Stonehouse Collection, *Material Service*.

xliv Oswego Times and Journal, January 30, 1856.

xlv The term "bateau" is French for a flat-bottomed , oar propelled craft commonly used on the Great Lakes in the 18th and 10th centuries.

xlvi Also known as the nation's "attic" for it's vast collection of "stuff."

xlvii Larry Molloy, *Copper Country Road Trips* (Hubbell, Michigan: Great Lakes GeoScience, 2001), p.68.

xlviii *History of the Upper Peninsula of Michigan* (Chicago: The Western Historical Company, 1883), pp. 511-512.

xlix *History of the Upper Peninsula*, p. 512.

l http://www.rootsweb.com/~miontona/history.htm

li Yes it is spelled right. The error occurred when the property was registered and it was left as waa.

lii Molloy, *Copper*, p. 73.

liii *History of the Upper Peninsula of Michigan* (Chicago: The Western Historical Company, 1883), pp. 255-256.

liv Angus Murdock, *Boom Copper, the Story of the First U.S. Mining Boom* (Calumet, MI: Roy W. Drier and Louis G. Koepel, 1964), pp. 20-26.

lv Lawrence Rakestraw, *Historic Mining on Isle Royale* (Houghton, MI: Isle Royale Natural History Association, 1965), pp. 1-2.

lvi Grace Lee Nute, *Lake Superior* (New York: Bobbs-Merrill, 1944), pp. 339-340.

lvii The term "bateau" is French for a flat bottomed , oar propelled craft commonly used on the Great Lakes in the 18th and 10th centuries.

lviii Ralph D. Williams, *The Honorable Peter White, a Biographical Sketch of the Lake Superior Iron County* (Cleveland: Penton Publishing, 1905), pp. 127-130.

lix Murdock, *Copper*, p. 339.

lx http://search.ancestry.com/db-lhbum07118/P58.aspx

lxi http:///rootsweb.com/~miontona/norwich.html

lxii http://www.telusplanet.net/public/dgarneau/indian20.htm

lxiii http://www.geog.umn.edu/faculty/squires/research/American_Indians/mille_lacs.html

lxiv http://www.themystica.com/mystica/articles/cannibalism.html

lxv http://news.bbc.co.uk/1/hi/sci/tech/911633.stm

lxvi *The Jesuit Relations and Allied Documents, Travels and Explorations of the Jesuit Missionaries in New France, 1610-1791*, Volume 35, LXXI.

lxvii James Edward Colhoun, William H. Keating and Stephen Long, *Narrative of an Expedition to the Source of St. Peter's River, Lake Winnepeek, Lake of the Woods, Performed in the Year 1823 by Order of the Hon. J.C. Calhoun, Secretary of War, Under the Command of Stephen H. Long, Major U.S.T.E.* ((Philadelphia: H.C. Carey and I. Lea, 1824), p.101.

lxviii *Charles R. Tuttle, Tuttle's Popular History of the Dominion of Canada, With Art Illustrations from the earliest settlement of the British-American Colonies to the Present Time, Together With Portrait Engravings and Biographical Sketches of the Most Distinguished Men of the Nation*, (Boston: Tuttle and Downie, 1877).p. 286.

lxix John Maclean, *Canadian Savage Folk: the Native Tribes of Canada* (Toronto: W. Briggs, 1896), p. 559

lxx Samuel de Champlain, *The Voyages and Explorations of Samuel de Champlain (1604-1616)*, (Toronto: Courier Press, 1911), p. 226.

lxxi Samuel Strickland, *Twenty-Seven Years in Canada West, or the Experience of an Early Settler* (London: R. Bentley, 1853), pp. 39-41.

lxxii James Edward Fitzgerald and R. Montgomery Martin, *An Examination of the Charter and Proceedings of he Hudson's Bay Company With Reference to the Grant of Vancouver Island* (London: T. Saunders, 1849), p. 154.

lxxiii Charles F. Thuing, *Cannibalism in North America* (Cambridge, Massachusetts, 1883), p. 36.

lxxiv http://www.fluffy.demon.nl/american/namtri.htm

lxxv http://www.tolatsga.org/ojib.html

lxxvi Frances Parkman, *Pioneers of New France* (http://www.gutenberg.net/dirs/etext03/pofnw10.txt) p. 379.

lxxvii http://www.bbc.co.uk/dna/h2g2/classic/A671492

lxxviii http://www.mayhem.net/Crime/ukraine.html

lxxix It is always "fishermen or fisherman" not the politically correct "fishers." The length some people will go to try to worship at the alter of political correctness is ludicrous. I will have not of such foolishness.

lxxx Stonehouse Collection, St. Joseph Harbor

lxxxi *Detroit Free Press.* October 31, 1906.

lxxxii Frederick Stonehouse, *Wreck Ashore, the U.S. Life-Saving Service on the Great Lakes* (Duluth: Lake Superior Port Cities, 1998) pp, 30-31.

lxxxiii Yawl, a small ship's boat; not a lifeboat

lxxxiv Storehouse Collection–*Myosotis* file

lxxxv *Annual Report, U.S. Life-Saving Service*, 1890, pp. 64, 80-81.

lxxxvi Frederick Stonehouse, *Women and the Lakes* (Gwinn, Michigan: Avery Color Studios, 2001).

lxxxvii *Women and the Lakes*, p. 59.

lxxxviii Stephen D. Tongue, *Lanterns and Lifeboats, A History of Thunder Bay Island* (Alpena, Michigan: Sarge Publications, 2004), pp. 45-46.

lxxxix Stonehouse Collection, Thunder Bay Island

xc *Alpena Argus.* February 7, 1912.

xci Stonehouse Collection, *Pewabic* file.

xcii *Alpena Argus.* January 3, 17, 1912.

xciii *Alpena Argus,* January 31, 1912.

xciv Theodore J. Karamanski and Richard Zeitlin, *Narrative History of Isle Royale National Park* (Chicago: Mid-American Research Center, 1988), pp. 81-82.

xcv Stonehouse Collection, Isle Royale General

xcvi Susan H. Godson, *Serving Proudly, A History of Women in the U.S. Navy* (Washington, DC: Naval Institute Press, 2001) pp. 1-3.

xcvii Godson, *Serving,* pp.6-7.

xcviii Godson, *Serving,* p. 13.

xcix Godson, *Serving,* p 23.

c http://www.nsgreatlakes.navy.mil/bulletin/womenofgl.html

ci http://www.nsgreatlakes.navy.mil

cii *Detroit News,* May 17,1931; http://www.nps.gov/apis/michigan.htm.

ciii Log of Marquette Harbor Light Station, NARA

civ Log of Marquette Harbor Light Station, NARA

cv Log of Marquette Harbor Light Station, NARA

cvi Stonehouse Collection–Whitefish Point Light

cvii Phyllis A. Tag and Thomas A. Tag, *Lighthouse Keepers of Lake Superior* (Dayton: Great Lakes Lighthouse Research, 1998).

cviii *Detroit News,* 1931; Stonehouse Collection–Alexander Carlson.

cix Whooping cough, also known as pertussis, is a bacterial infection of the respiratory system involving the voice box, windpipe, and breathing tubes. The infection causes irritation in the breathing passages, which results in severe coughing spells. The younger the child, the more serious the condition.

cx http://www.nps.gov/apis/mcclean.htm; Stonehouse Collection, Michigan Island Lighthouse.

cxi Tag, *Lighthouse Keepers of Lake Superior*; Stonehouse Collection–Sand Island Light; Luick File; http://www.terrypepper.com/lights/superior/sand/.

cxii *Nara,* RG 26; Stonehouse Collection–Lighthouse Keepers.

[cxiii] Donald L. Nelson, "First Woman Lightkeeper on the Keweenaw Peninsula," *Lighthouse Digest*, March 2002.

[cxiv] Stonehouse Collection–Gull Rock

[cxv] http://www.lhdigest.com/Digest/StoryPage.cfm?StoryKey=1255, Stonehouse Collection–Eagle Harbor.

[cxvi] Stonehouse Collection, Eagle River Lighthouse

[cxvii] Tag, *Lighthouse Keepers of Lake Superior.*

[cxviii] Stonehouse Collection, Sand Point file

[cxix] Stonehouse Collection–Granite Island

[cxx] http://www.itd.nps.gov/cwss/

[cxxi] Stonehouse Collection, Gibralter Light

[cxxii] http://hometown.aol.com/dlharvey/27thinf.htm

[cxxiii] http://www.lhdigest.com/database/uniquelighthouse.

[cxxiv] Candace Clifford, *Women Who Kept the Lights* (Alexandria, Virginia: Cypress Communications, 2000) p.186

[cxxv] Stonehouse Collection–Squaw Point

[cxxvi] Tag, *Lighthouse Keepers of Lake Michigan*; Stonehouse Collection–St. Joseph

[cxxvii] Stonehouse Collection, North Point Light

[cxxviii] http://www.terrypepper.com/lights/michigan/northpoint/north-point.htm; http://www.lighthousedepot.com/Digest/StoryPage.cfm?StoryKey +657, Stonehouse Collection–North Point Light.

[cxxix] Letter, H.C. Akely, Superintendent of Lights, to Professor Joseph Henry, Chairman, Lighthouse Board, March 19, 1874.

[cxxx] Stonehouse Collection, Calumet Light

[cxxxi] Phyllis and Tom Tag, *Lighthouse Keepers of Lake Michigan* (Dayton, OH: Great Lakes Lighthouse Research) n.p.

[cxxxii] Tag, *Lighthouse Keepers of Lake Huron*

[cxxxiii] Tag, *Lighthouse Keepers of Lake Huron*; Stonehouse Collection–Saginaw River Range

[cxxxiv] http://www.lhdigest.com/database/uniquelighthouse.cfm?value =285, Phyllis and Tom Tag, *Lighthouse Keepers of Lake Erie* (Dayton, OH: Great Lakes Lighthouse Research) n.p.

[cxxxv] http://www.ex-cult.org/General/identifying-a-cult

[cxxxvi] http://the-light.com/mens/samson/4/samson.html

cxxxvii People vs. Mills, Cal. 2., No. 334.

cxxxviii Robert C. Meyers, *Millennial Visions and Earthly Pursuits: The Israelite House of David*, (Berrien Springs, Michigan: Berrien County Historical Association, 1999), p

cxxxix http://www.fortunecity.com/emachines/e11/86/number3.html

cxl Philip Jenkins, *Mystics and Messiahs; Cults and New Religions in American History* (New York: Oxford University Press, 2000), pp. 55-59.

cxli Died

cxlii *Mystics*, p. 39.

cxliii *Mystics*, pp. 63-65.

cxliv http://www.eaec.org/cults/jehovahswitness.htm

cxlv http://www.rapidnet.com/~jbeard/bdm/Cults/jw.htm

cxlvi http://www.rapidnet.com/~jbeard/bdm/Cults/jw.htm

cxlvii http://www.rapidnet.com/~jbeard/bdm/Cults/jw.htm

cxlviii Perhaps Smith had a repressed sense of humor. Dropping the "i" makes Moroni into moron.

cxlix What is "Reformed Egyptian?" Is there an "unreformed Egyptian?" Why not have the inscription in English?

cl http://www.americanreligion.org/cultwtch/mormon.html

cli See the CBS News debacle regarding the apparently forged George W. Bush National Guard training documents.

clii *Milwaukee Journal Sentinel*, Milwaukee, August 1, 2004; *USA Today*, July 19, 2004.

cliii Mystics, pp. 32-33.

cliv www.rotten.com/library/religion/scienctology; Report,, "Lafayette Ronald Hubbard,"U.S. Department of Justice, FBI, April 14, 1967.

clv www.rotten.com/library/religion/scienctology

clvi Adkin, Clare, *Brother Benjamin; a History of the Israelite House of David*, (Berrien Springs, MI: Andrews University Press, 1990), pp. 6-7.

clvii *Chicago Examiner*, August 30, 1907.

clviii *Brother Benjamin*, p. 25.

clix http://www.rickross.com/reference/general/general552.html

clx Affidavit, August Holliday, July 30, 1914, Berrian County Building.

clxi *Brother Benjamin*, pp. 139, 156.

clxii *Brother Benjamin*, p. 156.

clxiii *Brother Benjamin*, pp. 79-80.

clxiv *Brother Benjamin*, p. 115.

clxv Which leads to the question, "If hot water bottles are not available, then resurrection doesn't happen?" As the Seventh Messenger King Ben should have shot up like an over done pop tart!

clxvi http://the-lightcom/mens/samson/4/samson.htm; http://www.rickross.com/reference/general/general552.html; http://www.swimdirectory.org/Israelite_House_of_David.htm.

clxvii *News-Palladium*, May 29, 1923.

clxviii *Brother Benjamin*, pp. 92-92.

clxix People vs. Purnell.

clxx "Dead Reckoning" is a way of determining a vessels location by using courses steered and distances run. The influence of current, wind, wave and compass errors are also taken into account.

clxxi David D. Swayze, *Shipwreck* (Boyne City, Michigan: Harbor House, 1992), p. 80.

clxxii Stonehouse Collection–Rosa Belle; *St. Joseph Herald-Press*, October 30,1917.

clxxiii *Brother Benjamin*, pp. 222-223.

GLOSSARY

Beach Apparatus–This term refers to the equipment carried on a lifesaver's two-wheeled cart. Usually it consisted of a line throwing gun (*see* Lyle gun), shot line boxes, sand anchors, hawsers, whip lines, shovels and related items. A life car was sometimes included (*see* life car).

Boot Top–The part of a vessel immediately adjacent to the waterline.

Bowline–A knot tied in such a way as to make an eye in one end of a rope. A running bowline is bowline made around the main part with the end of a rope and serving as a slip knot.

Brig–A two-masted vessel, squared rigged on both masts.

Bulkhead–A vertical partition which separates different compartments or spaces from one another.

Bunting–Flags or other pendants.

Canvas Patch–A temporary patch used for sealing off hull damage made of heavy canvas.

Clam Bucket–A device for moving bulk cargo. It consists of two scoops like a clam shell, hinged at one point so they can be opened when lowered into a pile of material, but will close when raised.

Daguerreotype–An early photographed produced on a silver or silver-covered copper plate.

Derrick Scow –A vessel fitted with a hoisting apparatus and able to handle cargo without assistance.

Fall–The rope which with the blocks comprise a tackle. The fall has a hauling part and a standing part, the latter being the end fast to the tail of the block. With some, the hauling part is simply the fall.

Flotsam –Floating goods or wreckage.

Fly–A three- or four-yard-long piece of cone-shaped bunting, sometimes used to signal preparation for departure or need for a tug.

Fore castle–The compartment in the bow set aside for living quarters of the seamen.

Fresnel Lens–Lighthouse lens designed and built around a series of glass prisms surrounding a light source in a lenticular configuration. Fresnel lenses were a major improvement over the previous parabolic system, and were made in France.

Grand Army of the Republic (GAR)–An organization of Union Army Civil War veterans.

Helmsman–The man who steers, the quartermaster.

Hoop Skirt–A woman's skirt stiffened with hoops.

Hurricane Deck–An upper deck above the superstructure. Often used as a promenade deck on passenger vessels.

Lamproom–Upper room on a light tower where the illuminating apparatus was located.

Lifecar–A small metal boat with covered decks that was used by the U.S. Life Saving Service to rescue victims from shipwrecks. Access was provided through a deck hatch and it could carry up to four people within its tight confines. It was employed in place of the breeches buoy.

Lifeboat–There are two meanings to the word. First, it is a generic term for any small rowing boat carried on a vessel for the crew and passengers to escape in, should the ship sink. It is also applied to a very special type of rowing boat used by the U.S. Life Saving Service.

Lyle Gun–Small line throwing gun used by the U.S. Life Saving Service.

Mass Copper–A term applied to any large piece of solid native copper.

Mizzen Boom Topping Lift–A rope device used to raise and secure the mizzen boom. The mizzen was the aftermost mast and the boom the wood spar used in conjunction with the mast and sail.

Oilskins–Foul weather gear, cotton garments waterproofed by repeated coats of linseed oil.

Painter–A rope in the bow of a boat for towing or making fast.

Pierhead–The projecting or offshore end of a pier or jetty.

Polygamy–Marriage to more than one spouse.

Punt–A small flat-bottomed boat.

Rigging–The ropes of a ship. The rope supporting the spars is called standing rigging and the ropes used in setting and furling sail are known as running rigging.

Schooner–Fore- and aft-rigged vessel of any practical number of masts above one.

Scow Sloop–A single-masted sailing vessel of light draft used in the local transportation of goods.

Shrouds–Pieces of rope fitted over the mastheads. They are made fast to turnbuckles or deadeyes and lanyards to the chain plates at the vessel's sides. They stay a mast at its sides.

Spar–A general term for a piece of round timber used for masts, booms, gaffs, bowsprits, etc.

Stove–A vessel broken in from the outside.

Timber Drouger–A bluff modeled sailing vessel engaged in hauling timber cargoes.

Thole Pin–Wooded pins that fit up in the rail of a boat to hold the oars in place while rowing.

Topsail yards–The spar crossing a mast horizontally from which the topsail is set.

Weather Earing–A short piece of rope secured to the grommet of a sail for hauling out the sail to its proper yard, gaff or boom when bending on or reefing.

Whip Line–A rope used by the U.S. Life Saving Service when rigging a breeches buoy.

Wind Wagon–An old term for any wind-powered vessel.

Victorian Era–The art, taste, thoughts and style prevalent during the reign of Britain's Queen Victoria, 1837-1901.

Volunteer Infantry Regiment–A military unit raised during the American Civil War.

Yawl Boat–A square -sterned wooden work boat, often carried at the stern of sailing vessels.

ABOUT THE AUTHOR

Frederick Stonehouse holds a Master of Arts Degree in History from Northern Michigan University, Marquette, Michigan, and has authored many books on Great Lakes maritime history. *Great Lakes Crime: Murder, Mayhem, Booze & Broads, Went Missing: Unsolved Great Lakes Shipwreck Mysteries, Lake Superior's "Shipwreck Coast," Dangerous Coast: Pictured Rocks Shipwrecks, The Wreck Of The Edmund Fitzgerald, Great Lakes*  *Lighthouse Tales, Women And The Lakes: Untold Great Lakes Maritime Tales, Final Passage: True Shipwreck Adventures, My Summer At The Lighthouse: A Boy's Journal* and *Cooking Lighthouse Style: Favorite Recipes From Coast To Coast* are all published by Avery Color Studios, Inc.

He has also been a consultant for both the U.S. National Park Service and Parks Canada, and an "on air" expert for National Geographic Explorer and the History Channel as well as many regional media productions. He has also taught Great Lakes Maritime History at Northern Michigan University and is an active consultant for numerous Great Lakes oriented projects and programs. Check frederickstonehouse.com for more details.

His articles have been published in *Skin Diver, Great Lakes Cruiser Magazine* and *Lake Superior Magazine*. He is a member of the Board of Directors of the Marquette Maritime Museum and a member of the Board of Directors of the United States Life Saving Service Heritage Association.

Stonehouse resides in Marquette, Michigan.